BRINGING IT HOME®
FRANCE

BRINGING IT HOME®
FRANCE

FORMERLY TITLED *BRINGING FRANCE HOME*

THE ULTIMATE GUIDE TO CREATING THE FEELING OF FRANCE IN YOUR HOME

CHERYL MacLACHLAN

WITH BO NILES

PHOTOGRAPHY BY
IVAN TERESTCHENKO

FROM THE BRINGING IT HOME® SERIES

CLARKSON POTTER/PUBLISHERS
NEW YORK

To Phillip,

FOR ALL YOUR LOVE AND SUPPORT
ON THESE MYSTERIOUS PATHS CALLED LIFE

PUBLISHED BY CLARKSON N. POTTER, INC., 201 EAST 50TH STREET,
NEW YORK, NEW YORK 10022. MEMBER OF THE CROWN PUBLISHING GROUP.

RANDOM HOUSE, INC. NEW YORK, TORONTO, LONDON, SYDNEY, AUCKLAND
www.randomhouse.com

CLARKSON N. POTTER, POTTER,
AND COLOPHON ARE TRADEMARKS OF CLARKSON N. POTTER, INC.

PRINTED IN CHINA

DESIGN BY DONNA AGAJANIAN

LIBRARY OF CONGRESS CATALOGING-IN-PUBLICATION DATA
MACLACHLAN, CHERYL.
BRINGING IT HOME—FRANCE : THE ULTIMATE GUIDE TO CREATING THE FEELING OF
FRANCE IN YOUR HOME / BY CHERYL MACLACHLAN.
INCLUDES INDEX.
1. INTERIOR DECORATION—FRANCE.
2. HOUSE FURNISHINGS—FRANCE. 3. COOKERY, FRENCH.
I. TITLE.
TX311.M235 1995
645—DC20   94-33143

ISBN 0-517-59806-X

10   9   8   7   6

ACKNOWLEDGMENTS

My warm regard for France has been deepened by all the wonderful people who opened their hearts and doors to me and gave me the opportunity to understand their culture. I give my thanks to:

Raphael Araud
Annick and Jacques Biolay
Daniel Bonnier
Michel Boutin
Paul-Henri Cecillon
Laura Colby
Beatrice and Yves Contejean
Bernard and Marie-Françoise
   de Wildenberg
Jean-François de Montvalon
Jean-Pierre Deméry
Stéphanie Deméry
Laurie Dill

Faith and Bill Doody
Luc Doublet
Étienne Dulin
Isabelle D'Ornano
Gerry Dryansky
Cary du Parc
Noelle Girard
Michèle and Yves Halard
Berna Huebner
Florence and Guillaume Jonchères
Lynn Kelly
Constance Konald
Jean-Louis Lasnier

Annie Laurent
Connie Leisure
Alain Markon
Dreda Mele
Françoise Mercier
Sylvie Mertens
Patricia and Patrick Pera
Jean-François Petit
Alberto Pinto
Carole Rochas
Carl Stibolt
Perrine and Jean-Yves Vincent
Margaretha Vriesen

To my French friends in the United States: Geneviève, Michel and Christophe Laverne, Christophe and Leslie Morin, and Virginie Biolay Wallace, for their enlightening insights. And to my France-loving American friends: Dori Cismowski and Eric Jones, Wendall Harrington, Marsha and Michael Lasky, John Levy, David Peterson and Paige Matthews Peterson, Nicole Pura, Maggie Simmons and Connie Wiley, who helped in every way possible.

The warmest hugs to "my gang"—whose love and support was the center of my universe during the many months I lived in Paris: Brenda and Gilles Charmey, Stéphanie de Montvalon and Vincent Gilles, Arnaud de Wildenberg, and "the girl next door," Sandy Sidey.

Bringing It Home—France was created simultaneously with *Bringing It Home—Italy*—an enormously humbling task that serves as dramatic testament to the fact that no writer is an island. I was blessed with much help and support and wish to extend warm thanks:

To Nan Talese for her encouragement and help on this project while it was still in the "notion" stage, and to Gay Talese, for his heartening remarks and support when I first showed him some of my writing.

To the "team": Ivan Terestchenko, whose brilliant photographs and sketches bring a true beauty and resonance to these pages; Bo Niles, whose extensive knowledge of architecture and decoration and whose lovely way with words allowed her to take my manuscripts for both books and imbue them with precision and grace; Annetta Hanna (who came into the world only hours after me and thus must share a certain cosmic relationship with me), who skillfully edited, carefully tended, and vastly improved these books; Howard Klein, Clarkson Potter's Art Director, whose wonderful talent and vision is exceeded only by his patience and diplomacy; Donna Agajanian, a gifted designer who embraced both text and photography and made them dance together; Jane Treuhaft, whose computer I envy and who adroitly led the design of both books to a handsome conclusion; Jeff Stone, my agent and on-line inspiration who has been there for me since the start, and his partner, Kim Johnson Gross, for her always helpful advice; and finally, Lauren Shakely, Clarkson Potter's Editorial Director, who believed in me and my concept for this series.

CONTENTS

INTRODUCTION

Is it possible to bring a country home with you?

This intriguing idea occurred to me in the most roundabout of ways. I started traveling regularly to Europe in the mid-eighties when I was supervising the Paris, Milan and London offices of *Esquire* magazine. I visited Paris four or five times each year, staying about a week each time. During the course of my workdays, I met and grew to know some wonderful people with whom I began to develop friendships. Before long, I was receiving invitations to dinner at their apartments in the city, then to weekends at their country homes. With each visit I found myself profoundly affected by the look, the feel, the sounds and the scents of French life. Something about this culture was nourishing a part of my soul that had heretofore been unattended.

Each time I returned to New York from one of these trips, I experienced a yearning, one I could not quite put my finger on. I loved my job and my life in New York—so it wasn't a case of wanting to pack my bags and run away to France. I decided that the answer, perhaps, was to try to make France a part of my day-to-day life back home. I decided to learn the language. I saw every French film that came to town. I read French magazines.

Still, I found myself wanting more.

Then late in 1991, I left *Esquire* and began a new career as a freelance writer.

An assignment in the fall of 1992 took me back to France. It was on this visit—waiting for a train in Normandy to return to Paris—that I finally realized what I wanted to do. I wanted to explore just what it was that made France France to me. Could I examine the French lifestyle and break it down into its elements—and then reassemble it? In short, was it possible to bring France home to America?

I arranged to live for a time with several families in different regions of France. I became a sponge, soaking up every detail of daily life: how the table was set, how the beds were made, how to search for the best fruits and vegetables at the market. I discovered that—just like God—French life was in the details. I realized it was indeed possible to re-create back in the States the essence of what nourished me during my trips to France.

Bringing It Home—France does not assume you have devoted years of your life to the study of interior design or haute cuisine. I focus instead on the more immediate questions: Why do French rooms feel so cozy? Why does the food taste so good? Why does one wish the night would last forever at a French dinner party? We'll walk through a pastiche of French homes, see how the French live and listen to their voices. Room by room, we'll observe how they create the environments they create, why they spend their time as they do and what values they hold closest to their hearts. And, through these images, you'll learn how to re-create in your own home the aspects of French life that most appeal to you.

Ivan took this photograph at the end of a day's shooting. We filled the basket with French treasures that are easily found almost anywhere: cheese, bread, wine, flowers, and brightly colored table linens.

How to **Use**
This **Book**

If someone asked you to describe yourself in a paragraph or two, you might find your-self making some generalizations that, although true, did not quite represent the full range of your character. You have many moods, many talents, many ways in which you express yourself.

Similarly, it is a challenge to describe the lifestyle of a country in one volume. France is a rich, diverse and engagingly beautiful country. She has many moods, many looks—and the talents of her people are expressed in myriad ways. One could easily fill a library with books describing all the nuances of *la belle France.* Indeed there are many such books describing aspects of particular regions of France that you will not find here: the lavender fields of Provence, for instance, or the half-timbered homes of Normandy or the magnificent stone châteaux of the Loire Valley—and more.

Instead, I have chosen to focus on the common threads that unite the various regions and styles of France. I limit these pages to only those elements of life in France that are transportable—those elements that, in effect, define the difference between incorporating elements of French style into our American lives and the mistaken belief that it is possible to "become French."

Bringing It Home—France is constructed like a house. After a brief overview of the elements that impart a feeling of warmth in the French home, the book is sectioned into rooms, beginning with the living room. In each room we look at the physical char-acteristics as they appear in both traditional and contemporary interiors. Where such aspects overlap—in the way a window is dressed, for example—the subject is only treated once.

I also look at the way life is lived in each room. In sections labeled "A La Française," specifics pertaining to each room are looked at more closely. In the dining room, for example, how is the table set? Sections labeled "French Classics" provide a background and description of quintessentially French items. In the kitchen, for instance, you will learn about copper cookware made in a small village in Normandy. And, finally, in sec-tions labeled "Voices," you'll meet some of the French men and women who opened their homes to me and shared their thoughts about life.

In short, *Bringing It Home—France* is a guide to enrich your life the French way. Unlike a guide, however, it does not impose a rigid set of rules. Re-create whatever strikes your fancy. Pick and choose according to your own tastes and desires.

After all, what could be more French than trusting your own sense of style?

WARMTH

TO STEP INSIDE A French home is to be enveloped by a gentle yet undeniably sensual warmth. Whether decorated in a traditional or contemporary manner, the interior indulges the senses. But like the French themselves—romantic souls constrained by refined intellects—the décor is often quirky, highly individual, and slow to reveal its many layers.

The thread that unites all French interiors, regardless of style, is the harmonious marriage of four interdependent elements: texture, color, light and scale.

Soft light tumbles down onto a collection of French guard medals. Note how the needlepoint screen enhances the feeling of texture. *Photo by A. de Wildenberg*

A Rich Sense of **Texture**

Mettre en relief is a French expression that comes from fine arts and photography; it means "to create depth of field" by layering the foreground, center, and background of a space. In terms of decoration, it is the interplay of textures on every plane and surface. For example, in a corner of a Paris living room a petit point chair and a couch upholstered in finely striped satin and viscose sit side by side on a Persian rug. The pillows on the couch are made from sections of an old tapestry. The walls are upholstered in a damask and the drapes are made from a small-motif jacquard.

The owners of this apartment have no desire to "match" anything, to use the same style of furnishings throughout, the same two or three colors or the same type of fabric. Rather, the value is placed on creating a harmony between all the elements of the room. (Interestingly the French don't have an exact equivalent of the English "to match." The word *assortir* is used for both an assortment and a match.) The family achieves this harmony by maintaining a fidelity and sensitivity to their personal tastes. Thus, if a kilim found in Istanbul and a Louis-Philippe–style sleigh bed appeal to them equally, they will work together in the same room.

To better understand the French layering of patterns and textures, think of the theater. One of two strategies may be followed: either a star stands out from a supporting cast, or an ensemble of players is created where no single individual outshines another.

In the star system, a dramatically patterned textile—say, a colorful cotton with an overscaled paisley motif—might be used to upholster the sofa. Several

In the Paris living room of designer Michèle Halard a rich sense of texture is created by the mélange of her many favorite fabrics and patterns, including kilims, toile de Jouy and petit point.

miniprinted Provençal cotton throw pillows and a quilted solid-color cotton-covered armchair could repeat, in supporting roles, the sofa's dominant color. Approached as an ensemble, a wool jacquard covering a loveseat might marry with a complementary tone-on-tone damask draped over a round table. These then might rest upon a Persian rug in a compatible low-key pattern.

In traditional interiors the fabrics used are very sumptuous. Among them might be richly figured damasks woven in the silks for which France is so famous; woolen tapestries, usually hung upon the wall, and their more intricately worked counterparts, the petit points, which are used for upholstery; and rich cotton or wool velvet.

In contemporary interiors the textiles are much less formal, but the surfaces are very high-relief. Coarsely woven linen and canvas, slubby raw silk, soft-napped flannel, quilted cotton and gritty sisal are popular choices. When a textile defers to surface interest, pattern and color become less of an issue.

Another important feature in the use of texture is the honor accorded by the French to the surfaces of their interiors. The textures of ceilings, walls and floors, as well as windows and doorways, are highlighted, from the aged wood of a burnished herringbone-patterned floor to roughly troweled plaster walls. These materials, in combination with unpolished stone, copper and bronze, all capture light in a soft manner and enhance the warmth of an interior. Although there are exceptions, such as the lacquered finishes associated with the Art Deco period, the French don't have an abundance of flat and highly reflective surfaces in their interiors.

Texture is created in many subtle forms: the branches, the dried flowers, the decorative motifs on the fireplace, and the weave of the fabric on the sofas all blend gracefully together to bring warmth to Dreda Mele's contemporary room. INSET: When using a single color, a delightfully rich sense of texture can be created. Note how well the high relief weave of the drapes complements the fabric on the sofa.

CREATING A RICH SENSE OF TEXTURE CAN BEGIN WITH ACCESSORIES AND DECORATIVE OBJECTS: A PLASTER BUST, A BRONZE SCULPTURE OR A COPPER PLANTER WILL ALL WORK TO CAPTURE THE FEELING. ON A MORE AMBITIOUS LEVEL, ONE MIGHT CONSIDER REPLASTER-ING THE WALLS OF A ROOM, LEAVING THE FINISH ROUGH; INSTALLING LIMESTONE TILES IN AN ENTRY-WAY; OR STRIPPING THE PAINT FROM A STAIRWAY BANISTER AND RESTORING THE FINISH OF THE WOOD.

TRUE **COLORS**

In prerevolutionary France, the colors favored by the reigning monarch were of great consequence. The king commanded absolute authority over everything related to the decorative arts, including the coloration of every object. Today, the colors traditionally associated with the French courts—burgundy red, indigo blue, deep green and lustrous gold—are still popular. A classically decorated room might incorporate several rich colors in the same textile. Although one color will be the dominant ground, the interplay of different hues creates the real story. And for further dramatic interest, *les couleurs unies*, solid colors, are put to work. For example, set among several multicolored upholstered pieces, a single chair or loveseat will be covered in an opera red or cobalt blue.

In many of the grander homes in France, families continue the practice of decorating different rooms, particularly bedrooms, in a signature color. A guest in a château may hear she will be staying in the blue bedroom, or meeting for drinks in the green drawing room. In these rooms the wallpaper, upholstery, drapes and rugs all feature the dominant hue, with other colors appearing only as accents. Of course, this approach would be difficult to integrate into a smaller modern home, where it would result in somewhat jolting transitions from room to room.

Inspired by the colors of her native Provence, Noelle Girard painted the walls of her home with rich velvety hues such as saffron, blue, ochre and rose.

A strong sense of play characterizes the French approach to combining colors—it's almost a high-wire act played out with pigments. There are no color wheels here, no right or wrong combinations. Rather, the process starts with one or two favorite shades, then comes the addition of a third or fourth, until the soul feels satisfied. Say you have a passion for burgundy red; you might select a burgundy and caramel-colored damask for your sofa. Your draperies then pick up the burgundy and add another favorite—teal—to the mix. A small Persian rug lying atop a caramel-colored carpet incorporates the burgundy, plus indigo, forest green and specks of butter yellow. Striped armchairs in burgundy and indigo complete the picture.

As a subtle variation to this use of color, many contemporary interiors play off one neutral or less-saturated color—such as celery, putty, faded red or pale blue—against another. Subdued values of the same shade may be layered to increase the richness of the interior. Draperies, for example, could be made in a wide vertical stripe alternating two shades of ecru. Additionally, it is quite common to use the *faux unis*, fabrics that appear from a distance to be of one solid color, but in fact are a subtle weave of many colors.

Flowers can be used very effectively to add color. Note how these deep yellow roses bring a richness to this room. RIGHT: Never hesitate to pair two strong colors: the deep red of the pillow works to bring even more life to the rich green damask covering the chair.

EVERY SURFACE IN THE ROOM IS A CANDIDATE FOR CARRYING A HUE: CEILINGS, DOORS, CABINETS, CORNICES, WALL MOLDINGS, BALUSTRADES, EVEN THE RISERS ON THE STAIRWAY. A SURFACE REMAINS WHITE BY DECISION, NOT BY DEFAULT.

Soft, low-wattage bulbs can be used to dramatic effect; a 15-watt bulb in an art deco lamp turns a small statuette into a bewitching figure. RIGHT: Natural light softly filtered through translucent drapes adds richness to interior surfaces, as in the entryway here and on the mantel display on the following pages.

TO CREATE AN INVITING AMBIANCE FOR YOUR NEXT DINNER PARTY, CONSIDER LINING SEVERAL CANDLES OF VARIOUS HEIGHTS ON THE MANTLE IN FRONT OF A MIRROR.

SHADOWS AND **LIGHT**

In eighteenth-century France the success of a soirée was highly dependent on the number of candles burning in the room. In the critical judgment of *tout Paris*, the mastery of lighting carried equal weight with the presentation of the meal.

While the advent of electric lamps has made the task easier, lighting a room is certainly no less important today than it was in centuries past. The French want to be flattered by light, not assaulted by it. To create this effect, they rely on sconces and lamps, accent lights, such as picture lights, and, always, candles. With the exception of chandeliers, overhead lighting is generally avoided.

The French are also accustomed to lighting with bulbs of a low wattage, 40 to 60 watts being the norm. This ensures a soft, diffuse glow throughout a room that, of course, flatters its occupants.

One of the tricks in developing a soft overall light is to use the reflections cast by mirrors or reflective surfaces. Aesthetically it is more pleasing to achieve illumination by placing a candle or bulb near a mirror than by simply increasing the wattage at the source. Traditionally, a pair of sconces was placed on either side of the fireplace: these would capitalize on the reflection of light from the mirror typically placed over the mantel and augment the radiance from the fire. Traditionally, too, chandeliers were placed so that they would be reflected in a mirror.

THE MYTH OF THE
OVERSCALED

The French have a legacy of decorating on a big scale. In the sixteenth century, François I converted an old hunting lodge in Fountainebleau into a château the size of a small village. It was dwarfed a century later by the little hunting lodge that Louis XIV turned into Versailles. But a curious thing happened on the way to the inevitable downsizing of modern residences. While the dimensions of the average room became smaller and more intimate, the time-honored tradition of bequeathing furniture and fine possessions to succeeding generations continued unchanged. If these possessions turned out to be a bit ample for their modern settings—*tant pis*—they were accommodated and showcased with respect. Thus the stage was set for the sense of scale that characterizes the French home today.

Enormous paintings, especially family portraits, are displayed in the living room, even if the walls allow for precious little breathing space. An armoire will be dismantled and reinstalled in a prominent position, even if it clears the ceiling beam by less than an inch. A sculpture that may have originally been placed outdoors can be squeezed into a corner of the library. Draperies are not limited to merely covering the window, but can cascade from the ceiling to puddle upon the floor. In short, the term "overscaled" is little more than an abstract concept, unlikely to trouble anyone.

Don't hesitate to use large objects in your living room. LEFT: Interior designer Corinne Wiley places a large antique mirror and gilded angel on an amply sized corner table and cloaks the doorway with floor-to-ceiling draperies. ABOVE: A trumpeting elephant and a crookneck lamp dominate the coffee table. RIGHT: Two large earthenware urns stand in delightful contrast to the delicate pedestal table and chair. OVERLEAF: Note the harmony in this room between the many large-scale elements.

THE LIVING ROOM

LOOKING AT THE BIG PICTURE—say, from the caves of Lascaux forward—the salon is a recent development in the evolution of the home. It was not until the eighteenth century that the proportions of a home's public rooms became sufficiently intimate to provide an appealing environment for conversation or a friendly game of cards. Before then there had been little or no differentiation among rooms; in fact, it

A lush combination of motifs and materials characterizes the living room of textile designer Patrick Frey. The golden-colored wall drapes, trimmed in plaid, are reversible to a full plaid. *Photo by Christophe Dugied/Stylograph*

Personal touches make
the living room espe-
cially inviting. A family
in Brittany proudly
displays their grandfa-
ther's hand-illustrated
hunting journal. *Photo
by A. de Wildenberg*

was common for guests to be received in the bedroom.

The salon eventually emerged in the 1700s as the most important and most carefully decorated room in the home. There, visitors could be graciously received and the art of conversation carefully cultivated. Indeed, conversation was such an important part of the experience of a French living room that the word "salon" came to take on an additional meaning. Sparkling gatherings of great intellects became known as salons and throughout the following centuries, from Madame de Tencin to Gertrude Stein, there was no higher achievement in Parisian social life than to play hostess to the luminaries of the artistic and intellectual milieux.

Today, the living room is still the center of life in the home. It is where guests are received, where the family gathers and where countless hours are spent in conversation. It also continues to be the most carefully decorated room in the house. It showcases the best of the family's furniture and art, and expresses their history. Prized possessions passed from one generation to the next are displayed with enthusiasm and flair; it is not unusual to find four generations represented in a family's salon.

Magnificently lush draperies are a hallmark of many French living rooms. Fashioned in deep hues of green and coral, this window treatment is particularly appealing.

GLORIOUS
FABRICS

The French weave fabric into their living rooms as if composing a vibrant, sensual collage. A striking aspect of this passion for textiles is the resourcefulness with which the French recycle their jacquards, tapestries, linens, velours and laces that have fallen into disrepair. Each is respectfully given a new life, usually having nothing to do with its original use. A damask curtain panel can be relieved of its frayed lining and transformed into an underskirt for a draped table. A remnant of timeworn tapestry can be trimmed of its most threadbare patches, then recut and welted for a pillow. Or a footstool can be recovered with a scrap rescued from an aged and decrepit Oriental rug.

Another fabric strategy is the use of slipcovers. These permit a change of outfit, much like clothing, for the season, for a party—for any excuse at all. Many younger homeowners, confined to a strict budget, use muslin, canvas and other inexpensive fabrics to rejuvenate old furniture inherited from relatives or salvaged at flea markets. In fact, the visual richness of any living room can be rooted in its lack of newness and perfection.

The French have a flair for experimenting with fabric, which allows for great flexibility in the decoration of a living room. Here, simple white cotton fabric has been used literally to wrap the oversize sofas. The twine remains as a whimsical ornament.

IF YOUR BUDGET DOES NOT ALLOW FOR CUSTOM-MADE SLIPCOVERS, CONSIDER OTHER ATTRACTIVE ALTERNATIVES. YOU MIGHT CUT AND PIECE SECTIONS OF FABRIC TO AMPLY COVER A SOFA OR CHAIR. TIE THE CORNERS, HANDKERCHIEF STYLE, BELOW THE ARMS AT THE SIDES, ALLOWING THE SURPLUS TO DROP TO THE FLOOR. TUCK EXTRA FABRIC INTO THE CUSHIONS. OR CREATE A CASING FOR AN ELASTIC RIBBON OR A DRAWSTRING AROUND THE BOTTOM EDGE OF A SIMILARLY SIZED PIECE OF FABRIC. SLIP IT OVER THE SOFA OR CHAIR, ALLOWING THE ELASTIC OR DRAWSTRING TO HUG THE BOTTOM. TUCK ANY EXCESS FABRIC INTO THE CUSHIONS.

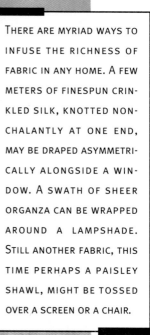

There are myriad ways to infuse the richness of fabric in any home. A few meters of finespun crinkled silk, knotted nonchalantly at one end, may be draped asymmetrically alongside a window. A swath of sheer organza can be wrapped around a lampshade. Still another fabric, this time perhaps a paisley shawl, might be tossed over a screen or a chair.

✦

FOUR QUINTESSENTIALLY FRENCH FABRICS

LIKE THE SIRENS calling to Ulysses, the French are drawn by the lure of fabric. Indeed, they celebrate it. Fabric is lavished over nearly every surface: it is stretched taut over walls, draped and swagged like a curtain across doorways, spilled over tables and cascaded from windows into lush folds on the floor. No single element defines the character of the French home more than the abundance and vibrancy of its fabrics. Here we look closely at four superstars in the field.

TOILE DE JOUY

Distinguished names are often borrowed for the products they inspire; such is the case with toile de Jouy. The word *toile* means cloth or canvas, while Jouy is the abbreviated name of a village, Jouy-en-Josas. Because of its proximity to Versailles, Jouy-en-Josas long enjoyed a steady demand for its products, which hap-

pened to be textiles.

In 1759, a local manufacturer named Christophe-Philippe Oberkampf invented a new process for printing on cotton. With his brother, Frederic, he opened a factory that

Toiles de Jouy

concentrated on printing patterns in monochrome, usually blue or red, on a white or dusky ground. Motifs were based upon detailed engravings of scenes that ranged from the pastoral to the mythological. The Oberkampf factory became a royal manufactory in 1783 and remained in operation until 1815, when economic conditions forced its demise.

Today, toile de Jouy is enjoying a renaissance, and many fabric houses both in France and in the United States are reinterpreting favorite patterns, not only in the traditional blue and red, but in other colors as well, including green, black, sepia and violet. Some toiles are even printed in reverse, white on a dark ground. Toile de Jouy is especially popular for bedrooms, where it is used for window treatments, wall coverings, bedcovers and upholstery, although it is often used in public rooms as well.

JACQUARD

Strictly speaking, jacquard is not a fabric but a weave. Named for its inventor, Joseph-Marie Jacquard (1752–1834), the term refers to the complex and intricate woven designs achieved on a special type of machine loom that

uses a series of perforated cards to direct the movement of the warp (horizontal) threads through the weft. Manipulating the configuration of cards and perforations enables the loom to produce countless designs. The complexity of the jacquard weave also ensures a tensile strength that a simple over-under linen weave cannot equal.

Jacquard's invention came about because he was appalled by the inhuman conditions imposed upon children laboring in the textile mills. Jacquard believed that child labor could be

replaced by machines.

Napoléon I underwrote Jacquard's new loom, and set him up with a staff in Lyons. The mill workers there first resisted his invention, for they believed it would put them out of work. Over time, however, Jacquard's machine proved to be their ally; by the time he died, more than 30,000 jacquard looms were in operation in

Lyons. Today many fabrics are still woven on jacquard looms.

Silk jacquards from Edmond Petit

PETIT POINT

Petit point (literally, "small stitch") and its heftier cousin, gros point ("large stitch"), originated as embroidery stitches and have been popular in France since the sixteenth century. They are worked stitch by stitch on a canvas that is often

prestamped with a pattern and held by a frame. Tapestries, by contrast, which these two needlepoints echo, are woven on a loom.

Before the sixteenth century, petit point was a craft practiced only by men.

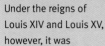

Under the reigns of Louis XIV and Louis XV, however, it was

Petit points from Braquenié and Casa Lopez

embraced as a pastime by noblewomen and ultimately became a critical element in the education of well-brought-up young ladies. But petit point came into its own as a result of the Industrial Revolution. Not only did more women find themselves in the position of having leisure time, but new methods of stamping patterns on canvas were developed, which allowed the rapid diffusion of designs.

A petit point is typically converted into a cushion or into the cover for the back or seat of a chair. Today there is a renaissance in petit point. Companies such as Casa Lopez and Braquenié have become quite popular.

INDIENNES PROVENÇALES

Block-printed cottons imported from India became highly popular in France during the seventeenth century. Featuring abstractions of small flowers repeated in high-contrast colors, these

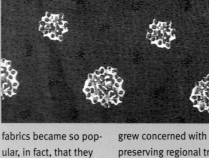

fabrics became so popular, in fact, that they were banned by the Crown, which sponsored its own textile manufacture. In France, cotton-print production was based in the town of Tarascon in Provence. Since Provence traditionally resisted the authority of the Crown, the people of Tarascon secretly continued to produce their copies of the indiennes, rejecting the

royal ban imposed by finance minister Jean-Baptiste Colbert in the mid-seventeenth century. After the Revolution, production was once again permitted but the patterns fell from popularity. It was not until the 1930s that a local family by the name of Deméry

grew concerned with preserving regional traditions and assembled an archive of 40,000 of the formerly clandestine printing hand-blocks. They opened a manufactory in Tarascon; their company, called Souleiado (which means "kissed by the sun" in the Provençal dialect), now markets indiennes provençales in many countries, including the United States,

where they were first imported by Pierre Deux.

Indiennes provençales are not exclusively miniprints; large paisleys, medallions and other florals are also popular. Patterns are typically brought into relief with stenciled outlines rendered in black or indigo, and they may be mixed together in terms of scale. The fabrics are widely used for table linens, in bedrooms, and as drapery and upholstery fabric in living rooms and dining rooms where a Provençal atmosphere is desired.

Indiennes provençales from Souleiado

À
LA
MÉMOIRE
DE
CHATA...
MA
PETITE CHATTE
BIEN AIMÉE
ELLE EST
ARRIVÉE
CHEZ MOI
MYSTÉRIEUSEMENT
LE SOIR DE NOEL
1925 A.D.
ELLE M'A QUITTÉE
LA VEILLE DE LA TOUSSAINT
1936 A.D.
MARQUISE DE CHARETTE

CREATIVE SOLUTIONS FOR WALLS

From the late Middle Ages through the seventeenth century, walls in the great French houses were hung with enormous tapestries or sheathed in embossed leather or heavy cloth. Drafts and cold were a major concern, and these methods of dressing the wall, while not highly effective, were at least serviceable. In the eighteenth century, the bourgeoisie's growing appetite for comfort merged with Louis XV's avidity for refinement, and the art of *boiserie* was born. *Boiserie*, or wood paneling decorated with moldings and carvings, proved a superior wall covering on many levels. With regard to comfort, it insulated against cold as well as noise. With regard to elegance, the endless options for carving, gilding and otherwise finishing its surface resulted in a far more refined and unified interior.

While the advent of central heating may have obviated the need for heavy tapestries and wood paneling, it didn't change the French desire for beautifully surfaced walls. Today walls are upholstered, papered, painted in imaginative trompe l'oeil or paneled and, in general, not allowed to "fade into the woodwork."

The rich atmosphere in this room comes not only from the deep colors used but also from the dense groupings of portraits hung on the walls. The obelisk on the desk is a tribute to the owner's deceased cat.

UPHOLSTERED WALLS

Wall fabrics reached a peak of popularity in the mid-nineteenth century during the reign of Napoléon III, when those who could afford it favored richly woven textiles such as satin, silk moiré, damask and velours. Many fabrics showcased motifs surely pleasing to the Emperor's sensibilities; medallions and crowns were among those held in highest regard. To add to the textural effect, pleating and swagging were popular measures.

Today, upholstered walls are again popular, although a much wider range of fabric is now used. Classically detailed and traditionally decorated homes in Paris remain partial to luxurious tone-on-tone damasks and velours; their more rustically inclined counterparts are likely to feature florals and Chinese-inspired prints. In contemporary rooms, canvas or natural unbleached linen tread the line between formal and informal. Occasionally, these are treated like the artist's canvas they resemble and are painted with murals or architectural features to add a trompe l'oeil dimension to the decoration of the room.

ABOVE: In the Paris living room of Carole Rochas a rich silk damask was selected to cover the walls. Note how well the wall covering complements the sofa. RIGHT: Interior designer Alberto Pinto specially commissioned this handsome striped damask fabric for his Paris apartment.

CONSIDER COVERING YOUR WALLS WITH ARTIST'S CANVAS. USE WALLPAPER PASTE TO AFFIX WIDE STRIPS OF THE CANVAS TO YOUR WALLS. THEN PAINT THE CANVAS IN A SOLID COLOR, OR GO A LITTLE FURTHER AND ADD STRIPES, CHAIR RAILS, BORDERS—ANYTHING THAT STRIKES YOUR FANCY.

PAPERED WALLS

Painted wallpaper originated in the mid-fifteenth century as an inexpensive alternative to costly tapestries and leathers for those who could not afford those materials. Ironically the first *papiers peints*, or wallpapers, had to be attached to panels of linen and then affixed to the walls. It is also ironic that by the mid-eighteenth century, "paper for the poor" had become fashionable and, appropriated by the wealthy, moved out of reach of the have-nots who had first embraced it.

The early motifs for paper purposely mimicked luxury textiles such as damask. In the mid-eighteenth century, however, retailer-turned-manufacturer Jean-Baptiste Reveillon was retained by Louis XVI to create original designs specifically for wallpapers. Reveillon and his successors continued to innovate, and as a result French wallpapers reached extraordinary levels of quality, beauty, and acceptance among the stylish elite.

Most French wallpaper continues to imitate fabric, and so papered living rooms in both traditional and contemporary homes have a similar appearance to those whose walls are actually uphol-stered. Florals, lyrical ivy and damask patterns remain very popular and can be used for the traditional living room, as can classic Chinese-inspired motifs. To decorate a contemporary interior, look for papers imitating grass cloths or faux finishes such as mottling or ragging. Tone-on-tone stripes are also natural choices.

TROMPE L'OEIL CAN BE THE SOLUTION
TO PROBLEM ROOMS. A NARROW ROOM
WITH TOO FEW WINDOWS AND TOO LIT-
TLE LIGHT, FOR INSTANCE, CAN BE
GRACED BY A PAINTING OF FRENCH
DOORS OPENING ONTO A SUN-
DRENCHED GARDEN, WHICH VISUALLY
DOUBLES IT IN SIZE. ANOTHER ROOM,
LACKING IN ARCHITECTURAL INTEREST,
CAN BE TRANSFORMED INTO A LIBRARY
WITH VOLUMES SO ENTICING YOU WANT
TO PULL THEM RIGHT OFF THE
"SHELVES." AND A WALK-THROUGH PAS-
SAGEWAY TO A KITCHEN, DEVOID OF
FURNISHINGS, CAN BE WITTILY TRANS-
FORMED INTO A PANTRY REPLETE WITH
"HOUSEHOLD NECESSITIES."

TROMPE L'OEIL

The French verb *tromper* means to deceive or to trick; *l'oeil* is the eye. Thus a trompe l'oeil is an optical illusion, a painting that creates the impression of three dimensions where only two exist, and deceives the eye into thinking that what is painted is real.

This technique of decoration is not limited to France. It was developed into a convincing art form by Italian Renaissance painters who painted dazzling vistas on the walls of their patrons' palazzi. Visiting French noblemen were mesmerized by these creations and imported Italian artisans to work in their châteaux. By the seventeenth century, trompe l'oeil and the companion art of faux finish were well established in France. Louis XIV was particularly captivated by a variation on trompe l'oeil known as grisaille (*gris* is French for gray), in which modulated shades of gray are used to imitate sculptural bas-reliefs.

The French have imbued the art of trompe l'oeil with their own idiosyncratic brand of wit and imagination. From the paintbrushes of professionals and amateurs alike spring fanciful images, from faux-draped salons in the Turkish style to cloud-banked celestial views. The murals painstakingly created by specialists are amazingly lifelike. But those lovingly painted by amateurs make up in charm and whimsy whatever they lack in realism.

A trompe l'oeil can bring a wonderful blend of whimsy and decorum to a room.

WALLS WITH **TEXTURE**

In the heart of the Loire Valley an old château is being lovingly restored by a talented and creative family who bought it in the mid-eighties. A corner room that serves as a painting studio receives the morning light and looks onto a tranquil pond. Its plaster walls had taken quite a beating over the centuries, leaving the surface rather similar to that of a peach pit. Yet instead of filling in the nicks and bringing the wall back to a smooth finish, the owners decided simply to paint the wall in its existing condition, character lines and all. They love the way the small, irregular depressions capture the light and create a sense of texture, a depth that would have been lost in a smooth finish.

In France many walls have this sort of rough texture. Made of stone or aging plaster, or punctuated by exposed wooden beams, their lack of cosmetic perfection is seen as an asset, not a flaw. Thus, if you are lucky enough to live in a house with such architectural features as exposed brick, exposed beams, stone or rough plaster, consider leaving the texture as is.

The owner of this Paris apartment has cleverly concealed storage cupboards behind wall panels designed to simulate the stone façades of the neighborhood's buildings. RIGHT: The attractive character of the aged plaster walls has been preserved under a simple coat of paint.

THE ART OF **FRAMING**

France may hold the unofficial record for the most framed objects per square foot of wall surface. A fantastic array of paintings, sketches, photographs and more are often hung only inches apart. The eye wanders from one framed work to the next—and the next and the next—in a never-ending journey of revelation and discovery. The shapes, colors and textures embodied within each piece work together to enhance the distinct personality of a room.

Creativity abounds in the frames and matting materials themselves. Frames range from classically carved and gilded to aged and weathered wood, from perforated and oxidized metals to finely tooled leather and other textiles. Mats include traditional rag papers and silk moirés as well as corrugated cardboard or wide grosgrain ribbon.

The French fondness for blanketing their walls with pictures from dado to ceiling traces its inspiration back to the magnificent *boiserie* of the eighteenth century. Thin strips of molding—often gilded or painted in a contrasting color—outlined the rectangular proportions of each piece of paneling, as well as the contours of doors, windows and fireplaces. Although it is rare to find real *boiserie* today, the practice of applying frame molding directly onto walls is very popular.

LEFT: Two appealing examples of densely grouped artwork. OVERLEAF: This type of frame molding is often featured on classically decorated French walls and is easy to re-create.

RE-CREATING THE FEELING OF *BOISERIE* THROUGH THE USE OF FRAME MOLDING CAN BE A RELATIVELY INEXPENSIVE AND UNCOMPLICATED PROCESS. FIRST, EVALUATE THE WALL SPACE YOU WANT TO "PANEL," DRAWING INSPIRATION FROM PHOTOGRAPHS OF CLASSICALLY DECORATED FRENCH HOMES OR CHÂTEAUX. THEN MAP OUT A DESIGN. GENERALLY, LONG WALLS ARE DIVIDED INTO THREE PARTS, WITH A LARGE CENTER SECTION THAT CAN ENCOMPASS BIG PAINTINGS AND TWO FLANKING RECTANGLES. THESE THREE SECTIONS ARE SUBSEQUENTLY DIVIDED IN TWO HORIZONTALLY. THE UPPER SECTION RUNS FROM JUST BELOW THE CEILING TO JUST BELOW CHAIR-RAIL HEIGHT; THE LOWER PORTION STARTS ABOUT 6 TO 8 INCHES BELOW THE UPPER "FRAME" AND RUNS TO 6 TO 8 INCHES ABOVE THE BASEBOARD. ON SMALLER STRETCHES OF WALL YOU WILL NEED TO PLAY WITH THE WIDTH OF THE FRAMES UNTIL THE PROPORTIONS FEEL RIGHT FOR THE SPACE. PURCHASE FRAME MOLDING (ABOUT $3/4$ TO $1^1/4$ INCHES WIDE) FROM A HARDWARE OR HOME IMPROVEMENT STORE. HAVE LENGTHS CUT AND CORNERS MITERED TO MEET YOUR NEEDS. PAINT THE MOLDING THE SAME COLOR AS YOUR WALLS, A SLIGHTLY DARKER OR LIGHTER VALUE OF THE SAME COLOR OR A CONTRASTING COLOR. FINALLY, ATTACH THE MOLDING TO THE WALLS FOLLOWING THE CONTOURS OF YOUR PLAN.

THE
WELL-DRESSED
WINDOW

In France, living room windows without drapes are about as common as theaters without stage curtains. They exist but they are certainly not the rule. Rather, the window is a point where the passions for fabric, drama and sensuality converge. The masterful techniques of cutting and draping that so characterize French couture are carried with equal dexterity to the window. Masses of material billow from rods and melt into soft mounds when they meet the floor.

In traditionally decorated living rooms, windows receive not one but two sets of draperies. The inner set, called a *voilage* (from the word for net), comprises a pair of sheer veils of fabric. In the nineteenth century these were often made of finely embroidered organdy, but today they tend to be simple panels of taffeta, linen or cotton. The *voilage* allows light to enter while preserving privacy. A recent variation is the *sous-rideau*, or undercurtain, made of a soft-hued, translucent silk or synthetic facsimile. When closed, the *sous-rideaux* bathe the room in an opalescent tint. When drawn to the sides and secured by tiebacks, they provide a sumptuous foundation for the outer dressings.

In contemporary homes and in smaller apartments, the French prefer a single

In the classic French style, these luxuriously proportioned draperies cascade from the ceiling to form soft mounds on the floor.

layer of draperies. Depending upon the size and character of the room, the type of material selected for the window will vary. In rooms where both space and budget are restricted, there is a tendency to keep the draperies very simple and diaphanous, using perhaps a light cotton or muslin. In larger rooms there are many variations to the passion for length and volume. Finely textured silks, lightweight damasks and *tissu surpiqué*—fabric in which an allover design has been quilted—are some of the fabrics that add an element of drama and refinement to the décor. Where two layers of curtains are used, the outer layer is made from more luxurious fabrics, such as a heavyweight damask or a thick, slubby raw silk that is lined and interfaced for extra body.

The top, or heading, of the drapery is indeed most often the "French" pleat. A threefold pleat, it is fastened to the drapery hardware with a pin-on hook that tucks into the pleat and is then inserted through a ring. The rings may be attached to larger rings that encircle the rod, or they may run along a track in a conventional traverse-rod-and-pulley system.

One of the most delightful evolutions in the French art of drapery in recent years is the clever manner in which drapes are hung. Rods designed in materials such as wrought iron or burnished steel, as well as in traditional polished brass and wood, are being accented with idiosyncratic, often eccentrically shaped finials. It is not uncommon to find a pair of seemingly windswept wrought-iron leaves or coiled serpents or gilded arrowheads

Elegant white draperies make a magnificent sweep along the arched windows leading to the garden. BELOW: A peach-toned *sous-rideau* brilliantly complements the drapery fabric.

protruding from either end of a rod.

There are many options for hanging curtains. The traditional pleated heading may be replaced with a series of straps in a matching or coordinated fabric or grosgrain ribbon. The curtains might be simply knotted around the rod, or tied to generously scaled rings in romantic bows. Sometimes, oversized grommets are punched along the top of the curtain, which is then drawn straight across the rod without any added furbelows. Alternatively, metal clamps are fastened at one end along the heading and snapped over the rod at the other.

Adding even more to the decoration of the window is the art of passementerie. These ornamental trims were traditionally made from silk and are now made as well from viscose, hemp, wool and cotton. Under the reigns of Louis XV and Louis XVI and during the Second Empire, wonderfully luxurious *glands*, or tassels, were fabricated by the most talented artisans of the day, using sumptuous materials and intricate knotting techniques. Today, large tassels still drape from curtain tiebacks. Smaller versions of these tassels can be used as a fringe lining the length of a curtain's edge. Beautiful braids, or *galons*, are used to accentuate lines of the valences or of the draperies themselves.

The art of passementerie is still very active, evolving over the years to include more contemporary versions of the classic tassels and braids. Most trims, however, are found on traditionally treated windows; contemporary dressings tend to be left as is.

RIGHT: Decorative hardware adds interest to a contemporary window dressing. BELOW: For a festive occasion consider adding a garland of fresh flowers or ivy to the tieback. FAR RIGHT: Bold patterns like this plaid become even more dramatic in ample volumes.

IF YOU WANT A TRADITIONAL LOOK FOR YOUR DRAPERIES, CONSIDER ADDING A FLAT BRAID ABOUT 1½ TO 2 INCHES WIDE ALONG THEIR VERTICAL BORDERS. USING THE SAME COLORS, ADD ROPE-AND-TASSEL TIEBACKS.

CREATING A
PERSONAL STYLE

Personal style works when it is, in fact, personal. The common thread running through all beautiful French interiors is the deep commitment found among their owners to follow their instincts. "You must never hesitate to fill your home with things you love—a souvenir shell from the seaside, a painting you received as a gift, the carpet you found at a flea market—everything that is beautiful will marry well," says Michèle Halard, a designer of textiles, tableware and furniture and co-owner with her husband, Yves, of the Paris boutique Yves Halard.

"I think it is important that people not get too caught up in having a certain style. It is so limiting," agrees Isabelle D'Ornano, who with her husband, Hubert, runs the family's Sisley cosmetics business. "People should just do what pleases them and it will all work out." What pleases jewelry designer Carole Rochas is an apartment bathed in sunlight. "I have friends who prefer the mood of subdued light, but for me there's nothing like a room brimming with the warmth of the sun. And when the sun finally goes down, there is nothing I like more than lots of candlelight."

The French women and men who welcomed me into their homes march only to the beat of their own drummer. They feel no urgency to follow rules, to make sure things match or to have a home decorated within any particular time frame. Interior design is very much like wine: it is best developed slowly over time.

The French decide early in life what pleases them aesthetically and never wander far from the path. "I've always known my style," says Dreda Mele, who runs the Giorgio Armani business in France. "White and light colors have always been my signature. I guess if anything has changed it might be that I've softened a bit—I tend to put more objects into a room now." Isabelle D'Ornano admits that she doesn't "really like change that much. For example, when my curtains needed to be replaced, I replaced them with exactly the same curtains! I love lots of color, lots of texture, lots of family things around. I've always been this way."

Understanding the difference between "having things match" and "creating a harmony" is an important

RIGHT: Michèle Halard

part of appreciating French style. One afternoon I visited with interior decorator Patricia Pera, an American married to a Frenchman and now living in Europe with her four children. Pera has worked with both French and American clients and noticed that "Americans, in general, tend to feel more comfortable when everything matches. The French just seem to want things to work together. It's more a question of harmony than sameness." Pera likened the French approach to looking at a painting from a distance. "There is a range in the individual elements that creates a pleasing texture and makes the painting work in the composite."

Michèle Halard goes a step further and warns that an interior can become "paralyzed" when everything is too similar. "Two couches in the same room, for example, don't have to be the same." And she thinks it is a mistake for young married couples to register for just one

Carole Rochas *Photo by B. Fabiani*

pattern of porcelain, opting to collect fifty-two pieces of the same shape and design. "It seems so impersonal. We shouldn't have to standardize our taste—instead we should seek a marriage of many styles. In the blending we find life. Forty years ago I bought all my tableware at the flea market and even today, when I am designing for the table, I like to create a collection of plates, bowls and cups that are easy to mix and can be used for many purposes. The same bowl for soup, for tea, for cereal and why not for a little bouquet of flowers?"

One reason the French are comfortable with mixing things in their homes is that so much is inherited from previous generations. "When I'm working with a French family," says Pera, "there is no such thing as starting from square one. They begin with all sorts of furniture, paintings and heirlooms. You really feel the presence of the family and it's my job to create a seamless flow between the past and the present."

Identifying with family and homeland is inextricably woven into French style. Nearly every person I visited in France mentioned the importance of their family when talking about their personal style. Isabelle D'Ornano stitched a tapestry for the birth of each of her children and made them into pillows or furniture coverings. "I think that keeping the family as the top priority is the most important thing any of us can do to make a better world," she says. "The family is the building block of society."

Heritage is always woven into the fabric of personal style. Annie Laurent is the *maîtresse de maison* at Les Marquises, the ranch she owns and runs with her husband, Henri, in the south of France. Her home beautifully reflects her Arlesian background, from the collection of faïence with Arlesian motifs, to the bright printed fabrics that dress her tables, to the traditionally costumed Nativity figurines, or *santons*, whose outfits were made by fellow Arlesian Christian Lacroix.

Stéphanie Deméry, whose family runs Souleiado, and Noelle Girard, the owner of the Souleiado boutique in the Provençal town of Carpentras, also honor their Provençal backgrounds. While each has developed a style that is distinctly her own, they both place a love of Provence at the center of their lives. Noelle Girard, for example, hand-painted a ribbon of olive branches around her kitchen walls. She placed articles from the ancient Arlesian sport of bullfighting, such as a matador's *habit de lumière*, or suit of light, in cozy nooks and crannies. Stéphanie Deméry captured the colors of Provence in the family-made textiles and on the walls of her airy loft.

Any discussion of French style has to include the element of warmth. When I asked Michèle Halard what gave her rooms such warmth, she replied, "Life— life creates warmth. The signs of your

Isabelle D'Ornano

life should be all around: the newspapers you just read, the books you are reading, your letters and photos. Everything that is an active part of your life should be present in your interior. I guess I'm really talking about disorder; if things are too well arranged, it makes you feel like not touching anything, as if you were a foreigner in a strange land." I asked her what advice she might have for people who are trying to refine their own sense of style. "They should stick to their instincts, and not get caught up in what someone else tells them is right. Americans especially have so much available to them—even your language is rich with expressions and words from so many different countries. Go out and mix all sorts of cultures, and in the mixture you will find your own sense of style."

THE BEDROOM

IT WOULD BE HARD to imagine the president of the United States receiving another world leader in his bedroom—yet in seventeenth-century France this is precisely where high-level meetings took place. From the Renaissance until the French Revolution, the upper classes in France gloried in, and glorified, the bedroom. During this time beds were never used simply for sleeping. Instead, the bedroom was the place where the most important rituals of a life were enacted in full public view, from birth to death. Ladies of the

An eclectic mixture of fabrics, patterns and furnishings brings a cozy warmth to designer Michèle Halard's Paris bedroom. Note that night tables and bedside lamps are not matched.

court were accustomed to receiving company in their bedrooms; Louis XIV took that custom a step farther and received the entire court while reclining in his *lit de justice*. When Louis XV's mistress, Madame de Pompadour, removed the bedroom from the traditional but all-too-public enfilade in the mid-1700s, she instituted a new concept: the bedroom as haven and private retreat, as the intimate place it remains, in most cases, today.

THE BED: A PLACE OF DREAMS

To say that the bed is an important element of French style is tantamount to saying that Joan of Arc had an inspirational effect on people. While true, it hardly hints at the magnitude of the notion. The French delight in beds; they lavish almost as much attention on them as they do on themselves.

Over the centuries, the French have created dozens of styles of beds. The canopy bed, or baldachin, originated as a practical solution to a difficult problem: how to sleep comfortably in a cold, damp and drafty room. Suspending curtains on all sides of the bed created what was in essence a room within a

A canopy attached to the wall serves as the focal point in interior designer Corinne Wiley's bedroom. Note the attractive combination of two fabrics in the canopy and the silk tassel trimming. A dreamy trompe l'oeil balcony is a witty touch in this seaside home.

RIGHT: Often the ceilings in modern homes are too low to install antique baldachins. One solution is to attach the canopy directly to the ceiling and drape the fabric down onto the bedposts. FAR RIGHT: An antique baldachin is well positioned in an alcove.

IF YOUR BUDGET OR AVAILABLE BEDROOM SPACE DOES NOT PERMIT THE INSTALLATION OF AN ANTIQUE FRENCH BALDACHIN, YOU CAN RE-CREATE THE SAME COZY FEELING BY BUILDING AND DRAPING AN ALCOVE. PLACE THE HEAD OF THE BED AGAINST A WALL. USING PLYWOOD, BOX OUT A SECTION OF CEILING OVER THE BED ABOUT 16 INCHES HIGH AND 24 INCHES DEEP. PURCHASE ENOUGH FABRIC TO UPHOLSTER THE BOX AND SUSPEND DRAPES FROM EITHER END. DRAPES SHOULD BE LINED. TIE BACK DRAPES ON EITHER SIDE OF THE HEADBOARD.

room. When the hangings were drawn, the occupant of the bed was assured a modicum of warmth and, in times when bedrooms were shared, a modicum of privacy as well.

Historically, ownership of a bed, especially a massive canopy bed, was a measure of social standing, rank and wealth. Only the nobility were permitted a full canopy; other aristocrats had to content themselves with a partial canopy called a half-tester. By the eighteenth century, canopies defined the types of beds they crowned. These included styles still emulated today, such as the *lit d'ange*, with its canopy attached to the ceiling or wall behind the bed, not to bedposts; the *lit à la polonaise*, with a domelike canopy and billowy leg-o'-mutton curtains cascading from all four corners of an independent metal bed frame; and the *lit à colonnes*, with hangings supported by four bed-posts.

After the French Revolution, bed dressings, which had been associated with the excesses of the aristocracy, became less ornate. The *lit en bateau*, or sleigh bed, and the *lit de repos*, or day bed, neither of which has a canopy, were two popular introductions. Although during Napoléon's empire these beds tended to have a rather heavy, earthbound look because of their platform bases, beds thereafter were created in a much less imposing style.

One characteristic common to many French beds is their placement parallel to and against the wall, or within an alcove, a position that retains the feeling of enclosure and warmth, especially when the bed is draped. A version of the alcove bed is the *lit clos*, a bed enclosed by wood panels, like a bed-in-a-box. A *lit à la turque* resembles a couch with the two arms serving as headboard and footboard, and the long back, higher than the headboard and footboard, placed against the wall. A narrow canopy is attached to the wall. The drapings flow down and over tiebacks so that they rest on either side of the headboard and footboard.

Today, to accommodate the lower ceilings of modern dwellings, the frame of the baldachin is often cut and made lower. The fabrics used for the drapery and bedcoverings are very traditional: toile de Jouy, cotton *indiennes* or silks, often damasked or quilted. Fabric rosettes and other passementerie are frequently used on the tiebacks and borders of the canopy.

In many French homes where the decoration tends toward the contemporary rather than traditional, the bed is more restrained. Adopting a look associated with Scandinavian countries, it often consists of a good mattress supported by a simple frame and dressed with a deliciously soft comforter and two square pillows.

A dramatic mood is created in this bedroom by using the same toile de Jouy fabric for both the bed canopy and the wall covering. Note also the pleasing juxtaposition of the large oval frame with the right angles of the corner.

THE MODERN
BALDACHIN

The baldachin has inspired many modern interpretations that preserve the appeal of sensually draped fabrics and cozy intimacy without retaining the heavier, imposing scale of the traditional. The most notable changes in these modern baldachins are in the frames and fabrics used. The frame is scaled down to the dimensions of modern rooms and rendered in lighter woods, such as pine, or in metals, such as wrought iron. Lines tend to be spare; even the traditionally fussy *lit à la polonaise* is more delicately detailed, and airier in effect.

Fabrics chosen for these beds are lighter in weight as well, ranging from diaphanous gauze to a thin linen or cotton. Unlike the luxuriantly trimmed beds of old, newer interpretations tend to be tailored with a minimum of passementerie, or braiding and tassels. The hanging of the fabric upon the frame is likewise far less ornate. The fabric may be simply draped over the frame, fastened to plain metal rings encircling the traverse rods that connect the bedposts, or tied in bows made from narrow strips that match or coordinate with the hangings.

Clean, simple lines and contemporary fabric characterize the draped bed of designer Angès Comar. In this version of the baldachin, fabric is not extended across the top, giving the bed a more open feeling.

✦

HOW TO MAKE A BED

ABOVE: The French are not accustomed to the American penchant for fitted sheets, in part because of a singular element of bed dressing that is not well known in the United States, the *traversin*. The *traversin* is a long pillow shaped like a bolster that stretches the entire width of the bed. Positioned at the head of the bed, it may be used alone but is generally used as a support for a pair of bed pillows. The *traversin* is usually wrapped in the "head" of an extra-large bottom sheet; the sides of the sheet and the ends of the roll are tucked under the mattress. A *traversin* may be covered in its own pillow slip, often one that matches the bedcover.

A popular transplant from the Northern European countries, the *couette*, or down-filled comforter, is the bedcovering of choice in about half of all French homes. Some people use a top sheet under the *couette* (as seen here), but most simply encase it in a duvet cover, like a big, puffy pillow. This cover usually matches the bottom sheet; in France, the duvet cover often includes a tail that tucks under the mattress to hold the comforter in place. On washday the cover is removed and laundered with the rest of the bed linens.

The bed skirt, or dust ruffle, is an indispensable part of the bed's ensemble. Oftentimes it will match the bedcover, or it will be sewn up in a compatible pattern. Like its American counterpart, the bed skirt is not only a decorative touch, but an article of concealment as well; with storage at a premium, space under the bed comes in handy for storing out-of-season clothing.

BELOW: Traditionally bed linens were a requisite part of a bride's dowry. Wellborn maidens brought at least a dozen sets of beautifully embroidered bed linens to their marriage bed. The embellished hem, or turnback, of the top sheets was very deep, and folded back over the bedcover in such a way that it would not be concealed by the *traversin* or the pillows. Sometimes, the turnback would cover fully half of the surface of the bedcover.

Today few brides are able to assemble an elaborate trousseau of a dozen sets of embroidered bed linens. The love of linens has not waned, however, so even if only two or three sets are ordered, these will be of the finest Egyptian cottons with a soft 250- or 350-thread count, or antique linens from the flea market, made from finespun unbleached linen.

RIGHT: The ample, overscaled pillows usually seen adorning a French bed are known in the United States as "European squares." Measuring 26 by 26 inches, European squares are now commonly available in America, although they are usually marketed as accessory pillows.

In keeping with European custom, the square pillows are encased in shams that open at the back, rather than in open-ended cases, such as those used to cover standard American rectangular bed pillows. The shams, which traditionally were monogrammed or otherwise embellished, may hug the pillow closely, or they may be finished off with a flat flange or scalloped edge or ruffle.

Because the French like to display their pillows, shams and top sheet, they often leave the bedcover, if any, folded back upon itself.

ROMANTIC
WALLS

The reverberations from Madame de Pompadour's preference for intimacy can still be seen on today's bedroom walls. Under the reign of Louis XV the use of fabric to cover the walls became current, and it is still often found in French homes. Chosen to match the dressings used to cover and shelter the bed, this fabric is typically soft in color and lyrically patterned with nosegays or floral sprigs. Like the rooms it enhances, wall fabric is calculated to delight, to seduce—in short, to inspire an atmosphere of romance.

To create a traditional look in the bedroom, consider covering the walls with cotton *indiennes*, toiles de Jouy or percale, a lightweight textile similar to sheeting. Luxury fabrics like shantung, raw silk or silk damask are also wonderful choices, if budgets permit. The fabric chosen for the wall should coordinate with the bedcovering, but need not match precisely as it did during the time of Madame de Pompadour. These days, there are many fabrics to choose from that synchronize closely, creating related patterns within a "collection." Favored designs are still inspired by flowers or stylized vines and branches, and these patterns are also available in wallpaper, which make a nice alternative to the more expensive fabrics.

The soft colors and lyrical patterns on this wall covering and screen create a romantic feeling. Note the layering of many patterns and textures, which also adds to the warmth.

The fabric may be applied to the wall in a number of ways. It may be stretched across and glued directly to the surface of the wall or, much like upholstery, it may be nailed or stapled over a layer of padding. Either way, it can also be outlined at the ceiling and baseboard in a tightly braided quarter-inch trim.

To achieve a very rich and traditional look, you may also want to consider swagging the fabric. This application works especially well in a shallow alcove where the head of the bed is against the wall. Treat the top of the alcove just as you would a pelmet over the window, affixing swags and tails in the same fabric used to upholster the walls.

In contemporary homes, the bedroom walls are usually painted, then hung with quantities of photographs and souvenirs. Imaginative trompe l'oeils—dreamy cloudscapes and the like—are popular, particularly in children's rooms.

Stéphanie Deméry used a collection of blue and white fabrics from her family's Souleiado collection to create a delightfully fresh ambiance in her bedroom. Despite the fact that only two colors are used, the presence of so many different patterns results in an appealing visual richness. Note the draping of the wall.

WINDOWS IN
SOFT FOCUS

Like the windows in the public rooms, those in a traditionally decorated bedroom are often swathed in voluptuous folds of fabric that tumble down and pool upon the floor. Because the mood in the bedroom is lighter and decidedly romantic, the textiles used at the window are, like their counterparts on the walls and bed, soft and airy. The *indiennes* and toiles are very popular, although featherweight silks are often chosen for luxuriously appointed bedrooms.

By and large, the French take the same straightforward approach to hanging draperies in the bedroom as they do elsewhere in the house. The draperies are usually pleated, then suspended from rings or hooks attached to a traverse rod. In formal rooms the rod will be hidden by a pelmet. In contemporary rooms, the draperies may be replaced by tailored roman shades, or by slightly pouffed balloon shades. When privacy is not an issue, plain, diaphanous panels suffice.

Many bedrooms in France have been reclaimed from quirky, under-the-eaves *chambres de bonne*, or maid's quarters, lit by dormer windows. The absence of right angles that results from the eaves or dormers, however, poses no serious challenge. Slim rods may be affixed to the slanted ceiling, or may swivel out from either side of the window sash. Alternatively, a fabric square may be dropped, handkerchief-style, in front of the window, then knotted to one side.

Interior designer Alberto Pinto created a light mood for this bedroom window using a lace voilage and soft yellow-striped fabric for the draperies. RIGHT: Gauzy drapes blow gently with the breeze. OVERLEAF: Balloon shades in a delicate blue print dress the window in this bedroom alcove.

LEFT: Although the colors are deeper than those generally used in the bedroom, these draperies with a flounce on the top hem create a nice mood. ABOVE: Bright colors on the window complement the matador's cape. RIGHT: A Paris bachelor creates a masculine tone in the bedroom with draperies made from flannel, edged in a polished cotton and trimmed with star-shaped grommets.

INTIMACY ON A BIG SCALE

The bedroom serves as a convincing demonstration that "overscaled" and "intimate" are not, so to speak, strange bedfellows. Rooms of modest dimensions can be furnished with a few dramatic pieces and feel very cozy indeed. A large armoire and a luxuriously proportioned sleigh bed, for instance, may appear perfectly at home in an attic room, especially when placed in the company of an invitingly accessorized bedside table and sumptuous tassel-held curtains.

The bedroom is a wonderful place to experiment with large pieces that are easy to move around. Such movable pieces as a tripanel screen covered in fabric can be placed strategically to make a bedroom feel even more inviting and secure. The reflection from a tall cheval, or standing mirror, can make an empty corner come alive. A stack of oversized cushions can create an instant reading nook. Any or all of these will nurture a feeling of intimacy in the bedroom.

Never hesitate to use large objects in the bedroom. They will add to, rather than detract from, the feeling of intimacy. Here an amply proportioned standing mirror is in perfect balance with the king-size bed. Note also how the flowing bedcover and the full-length cape draped over the mirror add to the soft mood of this bedroom.

LEFT: Although her guest room measures a scant 12 feet by 10 feet, Corinne Wiley knew her antique *lit clos* would work perfectly. Holding little else beside a standing lamp, the room offers the coziest of atmospheres. ABOVE: A tri-panel screen placed behind the bed and a large, striped reading chair help make this bedroom feel more intimate.

ABOVE: Volumes of fabric and a cleverly fashioned garland stretching the entire width of the bed create a pleasing scale in this bedroom. LEFT: Covered in the same fabric used for the floor-to-ceiling draperies, this bipanel screen is strategically placed close to the bed for a sense of intimacy.

PLEASURES OF THE **BATH**

In France the bath is drawn to soothe and delight, elevating a simple necessity into an indulgent luxury.

This was not always so. The centuries that followed the fall of the Roman empire were marked by a fear of water, which was thought to cause illness. Although several kings of France were known "to take the waters," bathing was avoided. Bodily odors were masked rather than erased. Louis XIV constructed Versailles without a single bathroom, relying instead on a continuous change of clean shirts, on perfumes and on chamber pots to assuage his bodily needs.

Not until the end of the eighteenth century did private baths become popular. A century later the bathtub joined the commode and the bidet as a necessity in the home. Under the influence of Louis Pasteur, bathing was championed as a protective measure to counteract bacteria. But the French—sensualists to the core—never accepted bathing as simply a health measure. Curative, yes, but to the soul as well as the body.

Many elements are at work in this beautifully appointed bath to create an atmosphere of luxury and indulgence: the soft fabric shades on the sconces; the rich marble vanity; the ribbon-tied sachets; the apothecary jar filled with cotton; and a marvelous array of crystal perfume flasks. Note also the handsomely tiled bathtub enclosure that is reflected in the mirror.

The **Art** of Taking a **Bath**

While the frenetic pace of the modern world has taken over many aspects of French life, the bath is not one of them. Like take-out coffee, the idea of a quick shower has never caught on. In fact, most French homes do not have showers as we know them in the United States. Instead of a shower head attached to the wall, the French configuration includes a *pommeau*, or hand-held spray shower, which diverts water from the tap. In some cases the spray can be hooked onto a wall bracket, but in many instances the *pommeau* simply rests over the faucets.

To understand the French perception of the art of the bath, one must bear in mind that the objective is not so much to get clean as to get happy. Drawing the bath is a rite in itself, mingling hot and cold waters to just the right temperature and perhaps lacing the water with salts or perfumed oils. Terrycloth mitts are used to leisurely soap the skin with fine, hand-milled soaps, often capturing the heady fragrances of Provence.

The French have long been renowned for the quality of their cosmetics, perfumes and skin-care products—companies like Chanel, Sisley and Lancôme continue to dominate worldwide—and a strong tradition still exists of affording oneself the best care possible. French women (and men) do not hesitate to spend time and money on personal grooming: it is considered essential to well-being.

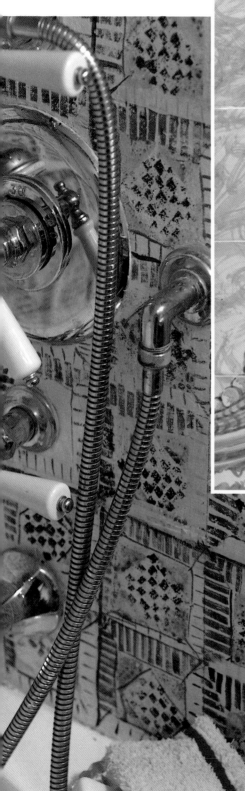

CLOCKWISE FROM LEFT: A glistening, hand-held spray shower is the bathtub fixture of preference in France. The "tiles" in this bathtub enclosure are the witty trompe l'oeil of a talented artist. Whimsical fixtures like this lion's head, swans or other animal forms are a coveted feature in French baths. The bath should not be a sterile place; don't hesitate to fill it with personal photos and other favorite objects. One can never have too many heavenly scents handy.

FRENCH CLASSICS

❧

THE BRIEFEST OF GUIDES TO FRENCH FURNITURE STYLES

Life rarely evolves with laser precision. Try as we may to label trends and styles, they seldom fit neatly into tidy packages. French furniture styles are no exception. They are, in the main, named after reigning monarchs, yet transitions from one so-called style to the next occurred so gradually that the characteristics of one overlap with the next. Many furnishings reflect this; they are hybrids, not pure examples of a particular style. Thus, although the reign of Louis XIV officially started in 1643, it was twenty years before the "Louis XIV Style" was fully developed.

Illustrations by Ivan Terestchenko.

LOUIS XIV—THE "SUN KING"

Reign:
1643–1715
Principal residence:
Versailles
Years associated with style:
1661–1700
Tone of the era:
Louis's ego is boundless. His rule is absolute; everyone at court is required to obey his command, without question, in everything from diet to dress. Louis orders enormous quantities of

furniture to fill Versailles; every piece is subject to the approval of his designated tastemaker, painter Charles Le Brun, all to assure a

homogeneous style befitting Louis' self-declared magnificence.
Characteristics of style:
Baroque. Luxurious carving and veneer

work incorporating precious metals and semi-precious stones. Rigorous symmetry and very rectangular silhouettes. Examples: heavy chairs and tables with X- or H-shaped stretchers. Elaborately carved decorative motifs, including suns, masks, fleurs-de-lis, animal forms and garlands of fruit. Dark colors preferred.
Introductions: The *bergère,* the commode.

Louis XV

Reign:

1715–1774

Principal residence:

Versailles

Years associated with style:

1730–1760

Tone of the era:

Intelligent and charismatic women like Madame de Pompadour and

driving forces in decoration.

Characteristics of style:

Grandly Rococo and more sculptural than previous styles. Curvaceous cabriole legs with arched feet enhance the lyricism of

Régence— Philippe d'Orléans

Duration of his regency:

1715–1723

Principal residence:

Palais Royal

Years associated with style:

1700–1730

Tone of the era:

The last few years of Louis XIV's reign grow intolerable. The aristocracy flees from Versailles to Paris to escape the oppressive pomp and circumstance of his court. Under Philippe, elegance, grace and intel-

ligence blossom. A wealthy new middle class emerges that desires a higher level of comfort in the home.

Characteristics of style: Lighter, more delicate, curvilinear silhouettes. Proportions, too, are more delicate and refined. Ornamentation, more restrained, is marked by a sense of whimsy. Motifs include the

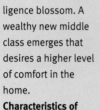

double C, palmettes, shells and especially scallops. **Introduction:** Caning for chair seats and backs.

Madame du Barry revolutionize the tone of social life. Entertaining becomes more intimate, more private. Comfort and elegance, not pretension and grandeur, are the

the furniture. Straight lines are broken by softly molded decoration. Lighter, paler colors and exotic woods are preferred. Decorative motifs include swirling scrolls, shells, flowers—especially bouquets and flowers in baskets—and chinoiserie. Marquetry is popular, as are porcelain plaque insets.

Introductions: Many new chair forms; also new styles of desks and the console table.

Louis XVI

Reign:
1774–1792
Principal residence:
Versailles
Years associated with style:
1760–1789
Tone of the era:
A return to classicism. Reason, restraint and an appreciation for the

countryside seem particularly prudent in light of brewing revolutionary activity. The discovery of the ruins of Pompeii stimulates an interest in Roman and Greek forms. Marie-Antoinette constructs her little "country folly" on the palace grounds, but it is hard to return to simple val-

ues when there is a monarchy to maintain.
Characteristics of style:
Rococo excess rejected in favor of symmetrical, neoclassical forms. Silhouettes become rectangular again; tapered, sometimes fluted legs terminate in a thimble-shaped foot. Decorative carvings are finely articulated. Mahogany is the preferred wood. Toned-down, grayed colors.

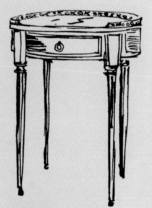

Motifs include palmettes, medallions, Greek keys, waves, scrolls and lyres. Porcelain plaques still popular. **Introductions:** The *demi-lune* table, the jardinière, new versions of the commode.

Directoire and Consulat

Years associated with style:
1789–1804
Tone of the era:
Fifteen of the most troubled years in France's history. The Revolution topples the monarchy. Three regimes follow in rapid

succession: the Republic, the Directory and the Consulate. It is a time of wild speculation, when consumption and speed of production are rewarded rather than craftsmanship.
Characteristics of style:
Reaction against the Ancien Régime. Silhouettes are severely simplified and austere, forms are clean and geometric.

Following the Revolution it is difficult to find skilled cabinet-makers and joiners; thus the Louis XVI styles are re-created in their basic forms and left largely undecorated. Light woods and subdued colors are preferred. Motifs

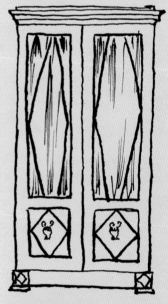

include stylized foliage, palmettes, masks, winged lions, as well as dragon feet.

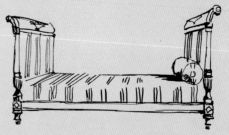

EMPIRE— NAPOLÉON BONAPARTE

Reign:

1804–1815

Principal residence:

Fontainebleau

Tone of the era:

Like Louis XIV, Napoléon controls every detail of his court. Inspired by empires of the past, he takes his cues from the pharaohs of ancient

Egypt, Alexander the Great of Macedonia and Augustus of Rome. Pomp rather than comfort is the driving force for life and furnishings. All traces of the lyrical and graceful French

styles developed under the monarchy are banished, so as not to conflict with Napoléon's supremacy.

Characteristics of style:

Majestic, rigorously symmetrical forms; straight, unbroken lines; emphasis on angles. Tables often supported on a massive central pedestal, thick columnar legs resting on blocks, or tripod bases. Strong, clear colors. The preferred wood is

mahogany. Motifs are singular to Napoléon: his signature bee as well as the monograms I for Imperator and N for Napoléon, both encircled by a crown of olive leaves. Also the eagle, stars, spears, rosettes. **Introductions:** The gondola chair and the sleigh bed or *lit en bateau*.

RESTORATION OF THE BOURBON MONARCHY

Reigns:

Louis XVIII, 1815–1824; Charles X, 1824–1830

Principal residence:

Tuileries

Years associated with style:

1815–1830

Tone of the era:

Following Napoléon's defeat at Waterloo, the two brothers of Louis XVI make a valiant effort to restore the elegance and refinement of the old regime and suppress the pomp and grandiosity of the Empire period. However, it is difficult to undo stylistic

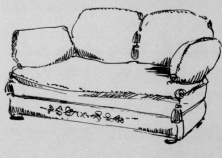

changes, and Greco-Roman influences from the Empire period continue to influence craftsmen.

Characteristics of style:

Silhouettes and lines become more refined and curvilinear. Proportions are scaled down. Blond woods are juxtaposed with dark inlays. Graceful moldings and bronze mounts are prized. Motifs include the swan, the lyre, acanthus leaves.

Introduction: The upholstered sofa, with the outline of the frame exposed.

Louis-Philippe—the "Citizen King"

Reign:
1830–1848

Principal residence:
Tuileries

Years associated with style:
1830–1848

Tone of the era:
The rise of the bourgeoisie to power engenders a divided loyalty between comfort and status. Not

quite secure in their taste, members of the emerging power class choose to disguise their new furniture in old forms inspired by Gothic art, the Arab world or ancient China.

Characteristics of style:
Lines and silhouettes, which had begun to lighten during the *Restauration,* become heavier. Pieces are less ornamented, due to the fact that production is now done by machine, which means less handwork. The

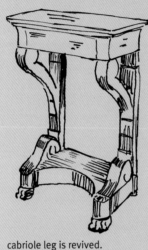

cabriole leg is revived. *La cuisse de grenouille*—the frog's thigh—is introduced as a decorative element where the chair leg meets the seat frame. Some gilded ornament, including the S-and-C scroll.

Introduction: Fully upholstered *fauteuils,* or armchairs, with no exposed wood.

Second Empire—Napoléon III

Reign:
1852–1870

Principal residence:
Louvre

Years associated with style:
1848–1870

Tone of the era:
Beginning of the modern age of science, industry and global economies. The Suez Canal is started. Europe is very active in its colonies. No new furniture styles are created, but details are copied from other lands and epochs— Gothic, Renaissance, Louis XV, Louis XVI, Regency, China and Japan—all at the same time. A frenzy of building and consumerism fuels an aesthetic melting pot which, ironically, results in a unique style of genuine appeal.

is preferred, often painted with floral motifs. Exuberant ornamentation. Favorite furnishings include the tilt-top pedestal table and small nesting tables.

Introductions: New seating forms including the pouf, an upholstered hassock or stool, and the *confident,* an S-shaped settee.

Characteristics of style:
A mélange of Renaissance, Louis XV Rococo and Louis XVI. Black lacquered wood

ART DECO
Years associated with style:
1920–1929

Tone of the era:
After the trauma of World War I, society is ready to spring back to life. An explosion of wealth and culture is witnessed. The intelligentsia flock to Paris; this is the period of Cocteau, Colette and Chanel, of jazz, of Hemingway and Fitzgerald.

machine technology. Reform movement turns to organic forms inspired by nature, and extols handicrafts. Thin, sinuous shapes and sweeping silhouettes make the furniture seem as if it were made from molten

ART NOUVEAU—THE MODERN STYLE
Years associated with style:
1890–1905

Tone of the era:
Vacillation between the status quo and the new. Automobiles, for instance, share the road with horse-drawn carriages. Also called the *fin de siècle*, this is the era of the Impressionists, of Proust, of the Eiffel Tower.

Characteristics of style:
Rebellion against

rather than carved wood. Motifs include writhing vines, leaves and flowers, usually distorted and elongated.

inlays use high-contrast materials. Exotic, expensive woods, such as ebony, and materials, such as ivory and mother-of-pearl, are preferred. Strident colors, or black and white. Geometric motifs, or motifs inspired by African art.

Introductions: Radio cabinets and phonograph consoles.

Characteristics of style:
Reaction to the stylistic excesses of Art Nouveau. Restrained, streamlined forms, often featuring rounded ends. Complex

THE
DINING
ROOM

UNTIL THE REIGN of Louis XVI the dining room was more a movable concept than a fixed point in the home. Meals were taken in any number of places throughout the house, including the bedroom, which was as much a public space as any other. During the second half of the eighteenth century, when furnishings began to be designed and arranged more for comfort, dining moved into a room specifically reserved for mealtime.

A centerpiece of ivy and moss perfectly complements the linens, glassware and porcelain that Michèle Halard has designed for her tableware collection.

The architecture was gradually modified to accommodate buffets and built-in cabinets, or *vaisseliers*, which displayed elaborate collections of tableware and serving pieces. Because public rooms ran in the connecting fashion known as the *enfilade*, the decoration of the dining room, then as now, was very much in harmony with that of the living room.

The pulse of the French dining room, however, quickens more around attitude than architecture. Dinner is an event for which one willingly invests hours to create a proper environment. Daniel Bonnier, the CEO of Groupe Bonnier Publishing in Paris, could be giving voice to a quintessentially French spirit when he declares that he does not simply invite people over to have dinner. "I invite them over to share life!" he says. At center stage is the table. "Sometimes I will spend hours setting the table," Bonnier continues. "I want it to be beautiful. It makes me feel good to create something special in my home."

"We have the word *saveur* in our language," he adds, "which does not translate easily in English." (The closest translation is "to savor" or "to relish.") "It expresses what we feel when we have dinner, the profound appreciation for all the riches life offers."

The layering of two tablecloths and the use of rich, dramatic colors give the French table its undeniable sumptuousness. Note that the bottom layer drops all the way to the floor and that, although these tablecloths were cut for a rectangular table, they work perfectly well on this oval form.

ABOVE: A *vaisselier* is a piece of furniture designed to showcase a family's collection of ceramics. Annie Laurent displays her ceramics with Arlesian motifs. BELOW: Candlesticks in the form of the bulls that are raised on the Laurent ranch. RIGHT: Many elements combine to create a soft, romantic atmosphere in Corinne Wiley's California dining room: coral-colored walls, cane-backed chairs, a tea rose centerpiece, real ivy "napkin rings," and the carved bookcase with a fabric-covered interior.

✦

HOW TO
SET THE **TABLE**

TABLE LINENS

When dining was still a movable feast there was a practical reason for a table-cloth to reach the floor. If Madame wished to dine in her *chambre,* the meal had to be rolled or carried in. A floor-length cloth hid the homely plank used as a table and its equally unsightly tres-tle base. Even after dining tables became more stationary, they were often crudely con-structed and thus needed the aes-thetic camouflage that enveloping linens could pro-vide.

Today, the art of dressing the table follows the guideline that pro-pelled Annie Hall into fashion histo-ry: layers are indispensable. Layered cloths, or *nappes,* give the table its rich look. There are three of these: a protective underlayer, usually a soft flannel sheet that pads the surface of the table; a generously cut underskirt that cascades in graceful gathers onto the floor; and a top that is generally tai-lored to drop about a foot below the table's edge. If the top is draped hand-kerchief-style over the underskirt, it is constructed so that its points hang two-thirds of the way to the floor.

When the occasion calls for a formal setting, the most direct route to ele-gance is white linen, white damask or, less frequently, white lace. Because a wedding trousseau traditionally in-cluded at least one complete set of one or two dozen white monogrammed damask napkins, the pure white table was, and still is, reserved for the most formal entertaining. For dressy occa-sions that are not quite so formal, fine linens in soft hues such as beige, celadon, rose or pale blue, or lyrically patterned linens such as those by the House of Porthault, may be brought out and set upon a solid-colored underskirt in a complementary (usually darker) hue.

Evenings with friends need not fol-low such strict protocol, however. When friends come to dine, the French indulge their natural flair for mixing and match-ing; whether the linens are old or new, inherited from the family or discovered at the flea market, bold in color or

TOP: Bright colors com-bine wonderfully for a casual dinner setting. The quilted tablecloth gives an appealing form to this table. (SEE RESOURCES)

Napkins may match or coordinate in a solid tone. The use of place mats instead of a tablecloth—a look inspired by American tastes but now becoming more popular in France—is appreciated if the table is of a pretty wood.

faded, they are combined to create an atmosphere at the table that is both charming and intensely personal.

When using bright, saturated colors, consider bold combinations—cobalt blue and sunflower yellow, for example, or kelly green with vermilion, or navy and teal. To achieve a dynamic effect, a geometrically patterned top cloth might be paired with a solid-hued underskirt echoing one of the dominant colors in the pattern.

For everyday use, or for relaxed weekend get-togethers, Provençal prints are perennial favorites, both in the traditional version or in new, laminated styles that suit outdoor dining. In these informal situations generally only one cloth is placed over the table.

PLACE SETTINGS

Setting the table is considered such an important part of French imagination and creativity that the French government sponsors annual exhibitions to promote the continued development of *l'Art de la Table.* Dazzling displays illus-

CLOCKWISE FROM TOP: Don't hesitate to combine bold primary colors on a table. A purist will insist on a white center as in this classic setting. White linen always makes for an elegant table. Adding a crochet trim enhances the setting even more. Select a charger in a color that will highlight a favorite color in your dinner plate, such as the deep orange in this Chinese motif. (SEE RESOURCES)

SET A TABLE FOR SIX OR EIGHT USING
DIFFERENT STEMWARE AND PLATES FOR
EACH PERSON. FOCUS ON HARMONY, NOT
ON SAMENESS—FOR EXAMPLE, USE
PROVENÇAL CERAMIC PLATES IN DIFFER-
ENT MOTIFS WITH A MÉLANGE OF MOLDED
GLASSWARE.

trating fantastical themes are organized; ballooning around the world, frolicking with angels, and the lure of the sea are a few examples. It is all part of "the table as theater," and the French bring an impressive level of talent to the exercise.

To the purist, it is absolutely unthinkable that food be presented on anything but a white surface. For this reason, fine porcelains are traditionally embellished only along and around the rim. If the center is decorated, it is simply with a medallion, or perhaps a few tiny flowers. Traditionally only a single plate was used at each setting, replaced after each course of the meal. Recently, the *assiette américaine,* or presentation plate—sometimes also termed a charger—has become popular. For formal settings the presentation plate will be quite simple, perhaps white or gold with a delicate trim.

When they entertain less formally, colorful tables are favored by the French. They ignore the purists' dictates and set out plates blanketed by strong motifs in bold colors. Presentation plates are chosen in shades that enhance and animate the top plate. Faïence (see page 108), with its bright colors and folkloric tone, is a popular choice for this type of table.

From course to course, variety is also the spice of table settings. It is increasingly rare to see the same service used throughout a meal. One pattern may be used for the *entrée,* then another for the main course, and possibly a third or fourth will be used before the end of the meal. Less common, but certainly not rare, is to mix two or more patterns during the same course.

FLATWARE

One notable difference between French and American table settings is the orientation of the fork and spoon. In France the tines of the fork and the cup of the spoon generally face downward so that the silver marks or engraving on the handle are visible. Just as in the United

OPPOSITE: The bright sunflower pattern is perfectly complemented by the colorful glassware and fresh ivy leaves. ABOVE: A Provençal print tablecloth is decorated with fresh olive branches. LEFT: Rich colors and highly charged patterns make for a festive table setting. BELOW: Not only patterns but figures, like this hunting dog, are popular on the French table. (SEE RESOURCES)

ever, knife rests in sterling, porcelain or glass are certainly a nice accent, especially if the table is casual and set with only one knife that is used for more than one course.

GLASSWARE

The French table parallels the American table in terms of glassware. Following the logic of the placement of flatware, glasses are placed from left to right in order of their use. To the far right is the water goblet, because this is the glass that is used and refilled throughout the meal. Immediately to its left are the slender white wine and rounded red wineglasses, then a small glass for a sauternes or vodka and lastly the champagne flute. During most dinners, however, only one type of alcohol is served; thus simply the water goblet and wineglass are needed.

For an elegant setting, the glassware will be made from the most delicate of crystal, always untinted so that the purist may appreciate the color of the wine. Finely etched crystal or crystal trimmed with gold makes for an even more sumptuous table. For more casual gatherings, or to create a fanciful mood, the French will often break ranks and decorate their tables with colored crystal, heavy molded glass, or thick, bubble-glass goblets.

ABOVE: Settings create a mood, like the rugged feeling of the Camargue. BELOW: The garland motif bespeaks classic elegance. OPPOSITE: The red tablecloth serves as a lush backdrop for etched crystal, gold-rimmed plates and fanciful candle holders. (SEE RESOURCES)

States, however, spoons and knives are placed to the right of the plate, knife blade facing inward, in the order of their use (the last used being closest to the plate). Thus, just to the right of the plate is the knife for meat, then the knife for fish, then the spoon for soup. The knife for cheese and the fork or spoon for dessert slide in between the top of the plate and the glasses, with their handles toward the right. For very formal occasions, when there is someone to serve the meal, the silverware appears as needed with each course.

The French custom of providing knife rests for their knives is gradually fading from the scene; how-

FINE
PORCELAINS

More than a million years ago primitive man stumbled upon the utility of mixing water with clay. While these first urns had an undeniable rustic charm, it was not until A.D. 1000 that the Chinese, working with a white clay called kaolin, began fashioning the brilliant, translucent objects now known as china. Three centuries later Marco Polo gave these creations the name *porcellana* because they reminded him of the seashells found in the Far East that were used as currency, which resembled the pigs known as *porcellino* in his native Venice.

Sea captains plying the spice routes from the Orient brought quantities of Chinese porcelains to Europe, using them as ballast for the lighter-weight spices and silks in their holds. These porcelains, in blue-and-white patterns, became so wildly popular in France, that, in a desperate attempt to rectify their trade deficit, the French sent out Jesuit priests to work alongside the craftsmen in Peking—and spy on them. Unfortunately for the French, the Chinese caught on quickly and fed misinformation to the good fathers.

What eluded the French, and the rest of Europe, was the actual kaolin. This ingredient in the Chinese "hard-paste" porcelain, mixed with feldspar and quartz and then fired at extremely high temperatures, resulted in pure white, exquisitely smooth, extremely durable wares. No deposits of kaolin were found in Europe until 1710, when one was finally uncovered in Germany.

A full half century elapsed before the French discovered kaolin within their borders. Ever resourceful, until then they had resorted to working with a "soft-paste" substitute that incorporated ground glass. Soft-paste porcelains are stunningly beautiful in their own right, with silky surfaces and intense, luminous colors. They can be scratched, however, by even a table knife running across the surface—not a winning feature for dinner plates. The chief producer of these wares, sponsored by the Court, was Sèvres Royal Porcelain located just outside of Paris.

In 1769 kaolin was at last discovered near Limoges, France, and a manufacturing frenzy was underway. In 1773 alone, eight new porcelain factories opened in Paris. Since the process of making porcelain was enormously cumbersome and costly, this would be the equivalent of eight new auto plants opening in one year in Detroit, complete with design studios and showrooms.

That the French were able to prosper during this wildly competitive time is a testament to their talent for design and decoration, and to their instinctive flair for the "luxury" trades. In an attempt to thwart the competition faced by its offi-

cial manufactory, the Crown granted exclusive rights to fabricate porcelain in fine colors and shapes to Sèvres. All others were restricted to the simple blue-and-white patterns already available from the Orient. Bucking government restrictions is nothing new to the French, and so manufacturers simply took their businesses underground and created wares they left unsigned. As a result, historians in the decorative arts, and even the most reputable antique dealers, have difficulty identifying many pieces of porcelain from that era.

With the Revolution of 1789, the carriage trade fell into ruins. The few manufactories to survive moved out of Paris, leaving only the decoration studios in the city.

When Napoléon came to power and set himself up as Emperor, he assumed an air of imperial luxury that included a love of porcelain. Celebrating his conquests in Rome and Naples, Napoléon favored motifs borrowed from Pompeiian frescoes and Roman ornaments as well as geometrics. With the rise of the bourgeoisie and the advent of the Industrial Revolution, porcelains became affordable to the middle class. Reflecting bourgeois taste, designs became heavier and were standardized; the most familiar motif, known as Old Paris, featured silhouetted vignettes of everyday life.

At the same time, exquisite pieces continued to be created for a discerning clientele. Eugène Marx of the Clauss family was one of the first *porcelainiers*

to set up a licensing agreement with Sèvres. For fifty years, from 1840 to 1890, Sèvres offered independent porcelain manufactories the right to purchase any model from its repertoire and reproduce it in unlimited amounts. Reproductions sold exceedingly well.

The porcelain industry continues to be very strong today. Manufacturers such as Bernardaud, Haviland and Ceralene in Limoges, as well as Christofle, Daum, Porcelaine de Paris and others throughout the country are creating new patterns every year in response to a healthy market.

When making an investment in fine porcelain, whether traditional or contemporary, you should make your selection based on the quality of workmanship. Is the surface of the porcelain smooth and uniform? Are the colors pure and even? Are the designs cleanly executed? Is the porcelain free from any sort of cosmetic blemish? If you can answer each question positively, you are considering an investment that will bring beauty and pleasure for a lifetime.

Nothing can match the elegance of a table dressed in white and set with fine porcelain. This service is a reproduction of Marie Antoinette's porcelain produced by Bernardaud. (SEE RESOURCES)

HOW
PORCELAIN
IS MADE

Hidden away in the 11th Arrondissement in Paris is Porcelaine de Paris, the oldest manufactory of fine porcelain in Paris. Just a stone's throw from the Place de la République, the company has been in continual operation since 1773, and indeed occupies the same premises, albeit updated, as it did at its inception. I visited with Chief Executive Luc Doublet and General Manager Paul-Henri Cecillon, who led me on a full tour of the operations and described each process in detail.

The "blanks" or plain white pieces molded to the specifications of Porcelaine de Paris arrive at the Paris atelier. These blanks have been fired once, but do not have any decoration. As they are unloaded, they are carefully inspected for any flaws or minuscule cracks in the body of the clay.

Designs created by artists are reproduced in multiples on a special film called a transfer. The archives of Porcelain de Paris include patterns from over two hundred years ago as well as contemporary creations. The craftsperson soaks the transfers comprising the pattern in water and carefully positions them on the blanks allotted to him or her during that work period. A protective layer on the transfer evaporates as soon as the oven reaches 350 to 400 degrees Celsius. A vent is left open until it fully evaporates, otherwise the final colors would take on a matte finish.

Each piece is inspected to assure the proper placement of the transfer. Then they are fired for two to three hours at 820 to 870 degrees Celsius (1508 to 1596 degrees Fahrenheit.) Pigments vary in terms of the temperature at which they are to be fired. Pushing the temperature too high weakens the enamel. In fact the entire process of firing is very delicate. The oven must be heated gradually over a twelve-hour period and then cooled gradually for twenty-four hours or the pieces might crack. After cooling, the decorated pieces are removed and carefully reinspected.

Some designs require decoration by hand before they are fired. In fact, 80 percent of pieces with a gold pattern are finished by hand. Gold first appears as a very black ink; it assumes its characteristic sheen only after it is fired. Some gold decoration must also be buffed. You can distinguish a hand-decorated piece by the inscription on the bottom, *fait main* or *fil fait par main*— made by hand or (gold) trim by hand.

The finished pieces are extremely hard and durable. Indeed, it is perfectly safe to place fine-quality porcelain in the dishwasher, unless it is decorated with gold, which may darken and discolor over time. The porcelain is packed for shipment to a destination in one of the thirty countries in which Porcelaine de Paris is sold.

THE STORY
OF FAÏENCE

The bases of most faïence plates are perforated with two small holes that allow for easy display. Just thread picture wire through the holes and hang on walls.
The decoration of faïence pieces can range from the elegant, as seen in the floral design above, to the simple and folksy, as seen in the two dinner plates from Quimper. OPPOSITE: Reservoir de Fontaine, Sancenis.

Although the pottery known as faïence developed into a distinctively French product, it originated from a type of tin-glazed earthenware crafted in the town of Faenza, in Italy, and specifically from the so-called *bianchi di faenza.* These pure white wares embellished with painterly, delicately drawn decorations became immensely popular throughout Europe just after the mid-sixteenth century. Tin-glazing, a technique whereby the clay is decorated with a lead glaze to which tin oxide has been added, was being crafted in Moorish Spain and southern Italy by the twelfth century. Majolica, as the Italians called this lustrous, high-colored type of pottery, was not limited to dishes; tiles, ornamental plaques and bas-reliefs were also manufactured.

Bianchi turned out to be far less costly and labor-intensive to produce than the majolica from which they evolved, and the process also allowed for elaborate molded treatments and openwork effects. As French artisans in Nevers, Rouen, Paris and Moustiers-en-Provence began to

improvise upon the *bianchi* designs, pastoral motifs and vignettes took precedence over the formalized scenes and patterns first copied from the Italian potters. Two forms, *faïence parlante,* with its calligraphic inscriptions, and *faïence patriotique,* came into vogue at the time of the Revolution; another, *faïence japonée,* was decorated with enamels in an Oriental manner.

Three centers of faïence stand out: In Rouen, potters achieved an almost lacelike decoration which they rendered over the entire surface of the plate; in Moustiers, craftsmen expounded upon a story-telling style, often focusing on hunting themes; and in Quimper, in Brittany, peasant figures, crowing roosters and simple floral patterns evolved into a distinct regional style. Quimper and Moustiers still thrive as producers of faïence. One can tour workshops, visit museums depicting the evolution of the work of local artisans, purchase wares or even place custom orders to personal specifications.

FLOWERS
ON THE TABLE

When it comes to their relationship with the environment, the French are at the same time both attentive and relaxed. Demonstrating great sensitivity toward the bounty of earth's offerings, they combine their flair for beauty with a *sans façons*—no fuss—attitude that results in

memorable settings and centerpieces for the table.

The scope of flower arrangements found in the French home is striking. In fact, "flower arrangement" is a term that should be taken in the most liberal sense, for many arrangements contain no flowers at all, nor are they necessarily "arranged." You are as likely to see strands of ivy laced around the bases of candlesticks as a classic bowl of roses.

The container you use and the manner in which you place the flowers and greenery should also be unfettered by convention. *N'importe quoi*—anything— can serve as the base for your creation. Consider looking beyond your collection of vases to jars, bowls, baskets—even a hollowed-out apple. And, instead of one large centerpiece, try placing several small arrangements around the table.

Consider using ivy, pinecones,
moss, olive branches, leaves, fruit,
vegetables, flowers cultivated,
dried, and wild—anything harvested
from nature's cornucopia. Ensure,
however, that dinner guests can see
each other. (SEE RESOURCES)

LET THE SEASONS GUIDE YOU IN DECO-
RATING YOUR TABLE. IN THE SPRING,
SCATTER SOME BRIGHT RED CHERRIES
NEAR THE BASES OF CANDLES OR OTHER
DECORATIONS IN THE CENTER OF THE
TABLE. IN SUMMER, GATHER SMALL WILD-
FLOWERS AND PLACE THEM IN GINGER
POTS AROUND THE TABLE. IN THE FALL,
WHY NOT HOLLOW OUT SMALL PUMPKINS
AND PLACE CANDLES INSIDE? AND IN WIN-
TER, CONSIDER LINING A BASKET OR A
SHALLOW COPPER BOWL WITH BRIGHTLY
COLORED CLOTH NAPKINS, THEN FILLING
IT WITH PINECONES AND DRIED BERRIES.

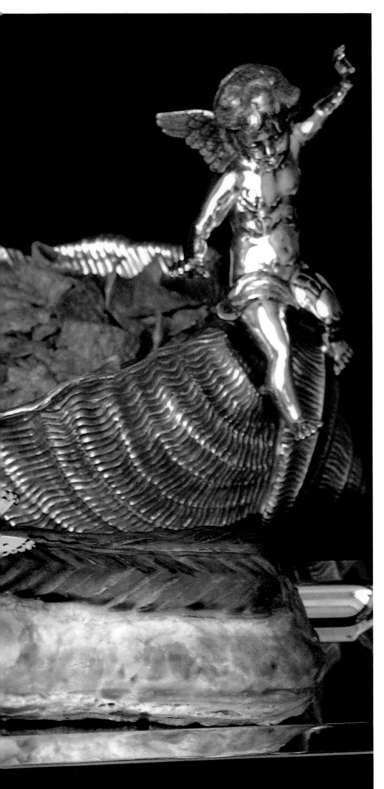

A HEALTHY SERVING OF **FANTASY**

The French may not exhibit the dry wit of the British, but never underestimate their sense of humor. Particularly when it comes to dressing the table, the French love to put a subtle spin on reality. Whimsy is often reflected in the shape of the serving pieces and ornaments used to decorate the table. A rabbit with a mischievous smile squats atop the cover of a terrine; a winsome mermaid curls along the handle of a serving spoon; oyster shells clasp a set of place cards.

But the real heart of the *clin d'oeil*, or playful wink of the eye, is the imaginative placement of these objects in relationship to each other. Looking around your home, you may be surprised by the number of objects you already own that might combine delightfully with the evening's menu. Consider setting free a school of crystal fish to "swim" toward the *fruits de mer*, or seafood casserole. Perhaps you have ceramic frogs that can ogle the figurine of a princess, or silver rabbits to guard a platter of stuffed cabbage. Anything that strikes your fancy and sparks your creativity can be transformed into a vignette for the table.

A ceramic maiden gasps at the giant cabbage balls, and an angel guards the silver boat of chips. It is not the place of the host to remark on these little *mise-en-scènes*. They exist for the guest to discover throughout the evening.

A LA FRANÇAISE

⚜

HOW TO SERVE DINNER

The typical French meal has six distinct courses; *l'entrée* (the appetizer, not to be confused with the American entrée), *le plat* (the main course), *la salade , le fromage* (cheese), *le dessert* and *le café.* At more formal meals there may be two *plats, a premier plat* of a fish accompanied by a white wine and a *second plat* of meat, such as roast lamb or beef, accompanied by a red wine. And, in place of coffee for the final course, many people are now beginning to favor *les tisanes,* which are infusions of herbal teas such as chamomile or verbena. On more formal occasions coffee is followed by after-dinner drinks such as cognac or Armagnac. (In the grand houses in times past, when the hosts wanted to signal that the guests should be on their way, the butler would bring in a tray of orange juice. Even today, a host may gently suggest fatigue by proposing fruit juice.)

While at first glance this seems like a huge amount of food, don't be misled. The French eat small portions and do not snack between meals. Therefore, while the French diet includes rich foods, the French themselves are quite slender and healthy.

L'ENTRÉE is served first, and traditionally consisted of a soufflé or foie gras. Today, the entrée is just as likely to be a soup, a light vegetable dish or a fish mousse. The entrée served here follows the traditional mode: it is a soufflé made from the classic hard cheese known as Gruyère.

LE FROMAGE is typically a selection of three and sometimes five cheeses. One will be a strong, aromatic cheese such as Roquefort, one possibly a goat cheese, and the last perhaps a local cheese. Here the Camembert is presented in the proper manner, with the first wedge already cut out. Only a knife and bread are used with the cheese.

LE PLAT, or the main course, consists of a meat or fish with one or two vegetables. Here guests are served veal forestier, a dish made with spinach. The dinner plate is never brought already filled to the table; instead, each guest is passed the serving dish and helps himself or herself.

LA SALADE, the third course, is usually just a tossing of fresh greens dressed with a vinaigrette. As with the main dish, the salad bowl is passed and the guests help themselves. Here, a ribbon of chopped hard-boiled egg is added to make a pretty presentation.

LE DESSERT may be a simple fruit dish, or less frequently, a sweet such as a tarte. After four courses it is easy to understand why the French generally conclude their meal with fruit. Here, fresh melons have been halved and filled with ripe red fruits of the season.

LE CAFÉ, the final course of the meal, is always taken in the living room, or living area if there is no distinct dining room. Coffee is served in a demitasse (literally, half a cup) and is taken black, although many people take sugar. On formal occasions after-dinner drinks may follow the coffee.

HANDS ON THE TABLE! AND OTHER KEYS TO GRACIOUS DINING

Table manners are like the rules of good grammar: ultimately you may decide to break them, but that should be done by choice, not by default. While most Western cultures share many of the same tenets of polite behavior, they differ in the degree to which those tenets are observed in contemporary life. The French continue to embrace the traditional rules of polite behavior. Thus while the following guide may echo many of the rules with which we were reared, they tend to be observed more rigorously in France.

SEATING. French and Americans do not differ in the matter of seating. The male guest of honor is seated to the right of the *maîtresse de maison*, or lady of the house. The female guest of honor is seated to the right of the *maître de maison*, or man of the house. The other guests are seated in the remaining seats, alternating men and women, with any other honored guests being seated nearer the host or hostess. Conversation is divided equally between neighbors to either side if and when the table is not involved in an all-encompassing discussion.

SERVING. Women are always served before men, commencing, as at formal dinners in America, with the female guest of honor and proceeding counterclock-wise around the table to the hostess, unless there is a second female guest of honor, who would be served second. Men are served in the same order. If there are no servants to pass the food at the table, plates are passed in this order, with the hostess quietly directing traffic. The lady of the house waits until all her guests have been served and then she begins to eat; this is the cue for everyone to begin.

WINE. A guest never touches the wine bottle or carafe and a wineglass is never filled to the top. It is the role of the host (or the server) to make sure all the glasses remain half full.

SILVERWARE. The fork is always held in the left hand, tines down, and is never transferred to the right hand, no matter what is being eaten. After cutting, the knife may be placed on the rim of the plate or upon the knife rest, if any. The point of the spoon is never lifted to the mouth, only its side. When the course is over, the fork and knife are placed parallel to each other and parallel to the table edge, so that their handles rest at "three o'clock." The tines of the fork face down toward the center of the plate, and the blade of the knife faces the fork.

HANDS. Both hands should always be visible, never placed on the lap. (This custom dates to ancient times, when the fear of a concealed weapon was no laughing matter.) The wrists are placed on the edges of the table, but never the elbows.

BREAD. Bread is served at all French meals, but it is generally not served with butter. Small pieces of bread may be used to push unwieldy vegetables onto the fork, but it is not polite to use bread to absorb a gravy or sauce. The most popular type of bread is the baguette, which is served sliced. However, if you are served a small roll, you should break off little pieces using your fingers, rather than lifting the entire roll to your mouth. If the table is not set with bread plates (although most formally set tables will have them), it is polite to rest your bread either on the edge of your plate or on the table just above the left side of your plate.

SALAD. Greens and vegetables are never cut with a knife, only with the side of the fork. It is acceptable to eat asparagus with the fingers, provided the spears are not too long and not inclined to droop.

CHEESE. Cheese is always posed, never spread, on a piece of bread. The cheese platter when passed will have a knife which you use to cut a serving and transfer it to your plate. Thereafter, use only your knife, not a fork, to cut smaller portions of the cheese and transfer it to the bread. If three types of cheese are served, only take one type. If five types are served, it is polite to take three.

FRUIT. A knife and fork are used to cut the fruit into quarters; then each individual piece is peeled separately, again using the knife and fork. A perfectly ripe peach may be peeled whole in the following manner: With the back of the knife blade, rub the skin of the peach all over; pierce the skin at the top of the peach; the skin will peel off easily. Fruit is eaten with a fork, never with the fingers. Grapes are the only exception to this rule.

SECONDS. The hostess may propose a

second serving of the *entrée* or the *plat*, but never of soup, salad or cheese. If any guest accepts the offer of a second portion, the hostess will follow suit and also take some. It is not polite to leave food on the plate, or to decline the first serving of any course. Plates for each course are not removed until all guests have finished.

THE NAPKIN. The napkin should be laid upon the table, not refolded, when the meal is concluded.

CONVERSATION. A sharp and witty mind is highly prized. The topic of conversation at a formal dinner is generally restricted to the arts, especially film, literature and the theater, or to politics. It is considered vulgar to speak about money, and unlike Americans, the French will not generally inquire what you "do."

✦

THE **ART**
OF
RECEIVING

nguage is a fascinating mirror for th
ues of a culture. The French attach
ch importance to the skillful enter-
ning of guests that a specific expres-
n exists for it, *bien recevoir*, which
rally means "to receive well." The ac
nviting guests into the home is an
it not lightly undertaken. Only whe
ie relationship has been established
an invitation to the home be ex-
ed. Thus, casual acquaintances will
: at restaurants, and social obliga-
will be addressed through other
ghtful courtesies, perhaps sending
rs or a carefully selected book.
ver the years that I have been travel-
and dining in France, I've discov-
hat while gracious entertaining
many of the same principles on
ides of the Atlantic, the execution
se principles differs widely. For
le, a "casual" gathering in Califor-
ght mean "Come in jeans," while a
" gathering
. might
No ties."

y to under-
g French
s toward
ning is to

Rich red walls, good
food and engaging
conversation ensure a
welcoming environ-
ment in the New York
dining room of Paige
Matthews Peterson and
her husband David,

read between the lines, to appreciate the role of polite modesty. When your hostess speaks of preparing a simple evening, she has probably spent several hours planning the "simple" details. (And, in fact, true simplicity does involve a rigorous discipline. Witness the designs of Frank Lloyd Wright, or the paintings of Mondrian or the 250 words of the Gettysburg Address.)

According to Dreda Mele, the director of Giorgio Armani in France, there are four keys to a successful dinner party: "First, always pour a good wine. Second, always serve good food. Third, keep things simple. And fourth, the hostess must be relaxed when her guests arrive. No matter what she has undertaken in terms of advance preparations, she must just stop and relax—and let the evening roll onward."

This belief in painstaking preparation followed by absolute relaxation is echoed by Isabelle D'Ornano, who owns and runs Sisley cosmetics with her husband, Hubert. She believes that it is the attitude of the hosts that creates an atmosphere in which the guests enjoy themselves. "I spend a great amount of time beforehand making sure everything is prepared, but once the party has started, I don't care if the house falls down! My husband and I want to enjoy ourselves and our guests."

Creating an environment that will stimulate lively conversation is essential to French hospitality. As in the traditional salons, this means gathering together an intriguing mix of people. "I always try to bring together friends from

different circles," says jewelry designer Carole Rochas. "I think they enjoy the opportunity to meet new people."

A hostess must be sensitive to the fact that a conversation takes on a life of its own, and may often bend the rules of etiquette to ensure that it not be interrupted. Dreda Mele believes even traditional customs should go unobserved if it means interrupting a good discussion. "It is impossible to reestablish the flow of a good conversation once you try to move people," believes Mele. "I would go ahead and serve coffee at the table rather

When receiving company, Annie Laurent often dresses in her traditional Arlesian costume as a sign of respect to her guests.

than in the living room to avoid cutting into a good discussion."

One point on which the French do not agree is the number of guests that constitute a "perfect" dinner party. Jean-Louis Lasnier, the chief executive of Fujesma, a market research firm, recalls the classic guideline: *Plus que les trois Grâces, moins de les neuf Muses* ("More than the three Graces, fewer than the nine Muses"). Therefore the options are three: to invite four, or six, or eight, since the number of guests should be even. Others, however, feel that a sit-down dinner of ten is perfect. One Parisian, known for her gracious hospitality, enjoys holding sit-down dinners for up to twenty-four.

The time-honored practice of using place cards is not universally embraced. Interior decorator Alberto Pinto believes that guests should feel free to sit next to whomever they choose. "Nothing about an evening must feel like an obligation," he says. "The guests should experience only pleasure." Pinto is also a strong believer in fantasy. He likes to create themes for his parties and enjoys decorating his table in a whimsical way. "I love to change the scenery for my friends each time they come to my home, with different colors and different foods. But, always very good wine!" he laughs. Some things are not negotiable.

Having an excuse to give a party is something Isabelle D'Ornano loves. "It might be the opening of a special exhibit, or a holiday. Whatever it is, it allows me to have a focus for creating an atmosphere." In contrast to many of her com-patriots, D'Ornano prefers to serve dinner buffet-style, as an "open house." "I tell people to come any time between eight-thirty and midnight. That gives everyone great flexibility. They arrive relaxed because dinner fits so easily into their evening plans."

Another reason she prefers buffets is that she feels a mixture of people from different walks of life mingle better when they are not constrained by a multicourse meal. A buffet allows her to keep accommodating any changes in her guests' day, right up to the last minute. If a friend wants to bring another friend, or if one of her children wants to invite a school friend—terrific, the more the merrier!

The type of food offered at a buffet should be simple, she adds. "I want everything to be elegant, but it must be able to be eaten with a fork. I never serve anything that would require a knife." Her menus generally include two or three warm and two or three cold dishes. One dish may lean toward the luxurious, perhaps tiny new potatoes served with caviar. The others, by contrast, might be simpler but mix exotic flavors, such as kasha sprinkled with finely chopped eggs.

Finally, of course, the main idea of receiving is for host and guest to have a good time. In this regard, Dreda Mele believes it is important to be surrounded by friends. "I think it is a mistake to invite someone to dinner just because one feels obliged to do so. There are many other considerate and appropriate ways to fulfill social obligations. Dinners are a special time. They should be shared with friends."

Et *VOILÀ!*
PULLING A
DINING
ROOM OUT
OF A HAT

Obstacles are in the eye of the beholder. To the French, the mere fact that one may live in a small apartment with no dining room—or even without a dining table—does not mean that a sit-down dinner is out of the question. Indeed, the smaller the space, the greater the dose of imagination and ingenuity, and, it seems, the more memorable the dinner. Depending upon the amount of space available, any one of three popular methods may be resorted to to create an instant dining room.

One solution involves a portable plywood table round that is set upon a sturdy side table or other base. Or a drop-leaf table, normally placed next to the wall, is pulled into the room and opened up. The last and easiest recourse is to convert a large worktable or desk into a dining table.

All three "makeovers" rely on tablecloths and underskirts for camouflage. One young Parisian trans-

Before and after photos demonstrate how beautifully a small work space or folding table can be converted into a festive dinner setting. RIGHT: A kitchen alcove table was transformed, thanks to a fabric remnant draped on the wall and sheet music used as place mats.

forms a heavy cream-colored linen sheet she discovered at a flea market into a table-cloth; another unfolds a large fabric remnant left over from when her mother re-upholstered her sofa.

Seating for this type of dining comprises either a set of folding chairs stored in a closet or an eclectic assortment of chairs gathered from various posts throughout the apart-ment. To dress up the eclectic mix, brightly colored cushions are placed on the seats, or a loose-fitting cover is slipped over each chair.

In lieu of purchasing an inexpensive dinner service for the sake of having a "matching set," many young people pre-fer to cobble together a medley of porcelain, faïence, silver and crystal gathered from the flea market, and mix them with treasures inherited from rela-tives. People's aesthetic prefer-ences generally guide them toward pieces that fall within a harmonious range: thus the resulting mosaic imparts a warm and festive atmosphere to the dinner.

Ensuite, candles are lit, wine—always a good one—is poured, delicious food is brought to the table, *et voilà!* a memorable dinner begins.

BEYOND THE DINING ROOM

Provence excepted, the weather in France is notoriously fickle. The warm, sunny days of summer are not to be squandered, and every possible opportunity is taken to eat outdoors on the terrace, in the garden or, ideally, at the country home. These meals are much less formal than those served indoors, but *il y a des limites*—there *are* limits. The objective is to simplify the menu, not to do away with the niceties. Thus, when dining outdoors the French may still serve five or six courses, but the food is earthier, more rustic and generally cool. A country pâté, a mélange of *légumes farcis*—stuffed vegetables of the season—or a freshly sliced Italian prosciutto with perfectly ripe melon makes a wonderful first course. The *plat* might be

Every opportunity is taken to dine outdoors when the weather permits. RIGHT: The table is set for breakfast. BELOW: Geneviève Laverne and I enjoy a freshly baked apple dessert. *Photo by M. Laverne.*

grilled shrimp or chicken. In the spirit of relaxation, the salad and cheese courses are often served together, and the dessert comes from the bounty of summer fruit.

Although a cool white wine is considered by most traditionalists the correct accompaniment to a summer meal, more popular in France is a chilled rosé, especially in the Midi, or south of France, where the vineyards that produce these grapes are concentrated. In fact the manager of one wine shop in Paris reports that she can barely keep rosé in stock during the month of July. Lighter reds, such as the Provençal Beaujolais or Brouilly, may also be chilled, and make a good accompaniment to summer meals.

Outdoor tables are decorated with a rustic touch, often with brightly colored faïence and heavier glasses, such as the robust bubbled-glass goblets made in Biot on the Riviera. Place mats may be chosen instead of a tablecloth, particularly if the table is constructed of wood in the refectory, or farm, style or if it is a painted metal table surrounded by the folding slatted chairs familiar from French parks.

It may be Italian, but prosciutto is quite welcome at the French table. Michel Laverne carves a perfectly cured ham for lunch in the Loire Valley. RIGHT: Note the robust glassware and bright ceramics. *Photo by G. Laverne.*

GARDENS IN SMALL SPACES

The French have an astonishing talent for creating a garden in any space larger than a handkerchief. Their passion for flowers and greenery gives rise to an imaginative array of microgardens. On rooftops, stoops, windowsills, terraces and in courtyards, all varieties of blossoms, shrubs, herbs and vegetables stretch toward the sun.

The key to creating these magical gardens is believing you can never have too many pots. Collect a menagerie of shapes, sizes and materials and place them in every nook and cranny of your available space. Fill them with geraniums, petunias, marigolds and pansies, or in shaded areas, with impatiens or cyclamens. Hang them from overhead, attach them to walls, put them up along shelves. Train ivies and other climbers along railings or trellises. Let plants tumble down exterior walls. Once you learn to think in terms of cubic space rather than linear space, your horizons will be limitless.

THE RESOURCEFUL FRENCH ART OF *POTAGER*—GROWING HERBS AND VEGETABLES IN POTS—IS A PRACTICAL AND EFFECTIVE WAY TO ELEVATE SUMMER MENUS FROM GOOD TO *WOW!* ON A SUNNY KITCHEN WINDOWSILL, OR IN ANY OTHER PLANT-FRIENDLY SPOT, TRY PLANTING A VARIETY OF HERBS IN SMALL TERRA-COTTA POTS: BASIL, ROSEMARY, THYME AND MINT ARE PARTICULARLY POPULAR AND NOT DIFFICULT TO GROW. IF YOU HAVE ADDITIONAL ROOM AND CAN TRELLIS PLANTS UPWARD, WHY NOT TRY TOMATOES, PEPPERS, STRING BEANS OR EVEN STRAWBERRIES?

Bountiful gardens can spring from the smallest of terraces and courtyards. The key is seeing your options in three dimensions.

CHILDREN

TO APPRECIATE the particular quality and rhythm of French daily life, it is helpful to take a close look at attitudes toward the family and, more specifically, toward children. In France, children are both adored and implored to live up to an exacting standard. Beautifully dressed and groomed, and trained from toddlerhood to observe social courtesies, children participate fully in the activities of family life, but in a respectful fashion that honors the status of adults in the household.

Young children in France spend hours each week with their favorite books. Here, Alice reads to her cousin Robin and little sister Fanny. The delightful figures of Babar and Celeste were painted by a teenage cousin.

Good manners are a must. Adults are always addressed as *Madame* and *Monsieur*. "Please" is never omitted from a request, nor "thank you" from a response. At dinnertime it's "hands on the table" (see page 118), and permission is asked to be excused. Even a youngster exuberantly chasing a ball in the park will stop to say "excuse me" if he or she accidentally bumps into an adult.

Children are lavished with attention and treated with the respect they are expected to give back in return. They are welcomed, for instance, onto an open lap at family gatherings and invited to join regular outings to restaurants. Their opinions are solicited with consideration, so that they always feel an intimate part of the adult goings-on. Yet an appropriate measure of reserve is assumed. If a conversation is taking place around them, for example, children are expected to sit quietly.

CLOCKWISE FROM ABOVE: A brightly decorated canopy bed is set up in Grandmother's Paris apartment for visiting grandchildren. A young mind is absorbed by a good book during summer vacation. The *Guignol,* the favorite puppet theater of every French child, is a fixture in many homes. *Photo by A. de Wildenberg.*

THE ART OF
LEARNING

Because the French place such a high value on intellectual development and on the art of conversation, schooling is taken seriously. The school day is long, often running from 8:30 to 4:30, and the demands of homework are rigorous. But there is perhaps nothing more symbolic of the support French parents give their school-age children than the afternoon ritual called *l'heure du goûter*, or snack time. In the late afternoon mothers line up at school doors awaiting their young-sters with warm *pains au chocolat* freshly baked from the neighborhood bakery; the chocolate-filled croissants are a delicious reward to celebrate the end of a demand-ing school day.

Because children are considered to have healthy intellects and active imagi-nations, considerable effort is made to provide an environment that encourages their curiosity. For instance, dolls, mari-onettes and small puppet theaters, all of which inspire story writing and story-telling, are fixtures in many children's playrooms and bedrooms. Books, espe-cially classics, are enormously important. Babar, the regal elephant king, and his lovely queen Celeste are particularly beloved, as is Madeleine, the eternally young but ever-wise little schoolgirl. And to begin to familiarize them with the great works of art, volumes such as the *Petit Musée* (Little Museum), exist for children as young as four and five.

The emphasis placed on reading, the cultural value of conversation and perhaps the relative unimportance of television—children in France generally watch television less than an hour a day—all have an important effect on the relationship between child and parent: they spend large blocks of time simply talking to one another. During a stroll in the park, it is not uncommon to hear children of five or six engaged in animated conversations with their parents or grandparents, discussing colorful historical figures like Napoléon and Joan of Arc, curiosities such as where thunder comes from, or simply recounting the day at school.

Magical worlds are created for children. CLOCKWISE FROM LEFT: Grandmother Sylvie has converted an old steamer trunk into a closet for her granddaughters. Peter Cary's antique baldachin shelters a troupe of stuffed animals waiting patiently for him to return. Traditional toys like wooden trains and teddy bears are perennial favorites.

HOLIDAY **TRADITIONS** FOR THE FAMILY

CHRISTMAS

In France the vast majority of the population is Catholic. Christmas is therefore an important celebration, both religiously and socially. In anticipation of the arrival of *le père Noël*, each child places his or her favorite pair of shoes near the fireplace to be filled with gifts. If the little shoes overflow—oh, wonder of wonders—*le père Noël* will leave larger parcels close by.

A favorite rite of the holiday season is the setting up of the crèche, or Nativity scene. Many families erect elaborate little villages, comprised of painted wooden or clay figures collected and passed down through the generations. The unwrapping of these beloved *santons*—which represent all the various townspeople of a village, as well as the Holy Family and the Magi—is a joyful occasion.

All family members seem to have their favorite characters to place in the scene. In some families, each child has a lamb, which is placed at a distance from the manger. Each day during Advent, the lambs either advance or retreat slightly, depending on how the child has behaved. The objective, of course, is to reach the manger by Christmas Eve. Much good-natured advancing and retreating goes on, but somehow all the lambs manage to make it before *le père Noël* makes his inevitable and invisible entrance.

Traditionally, the Christmas tree was

ABOVE: On this Sunday of the Epiphany, young Marion has found the porcelain piece that earned her the crown. LEFT: Two young sisters celebrate the Christmas spirit by helping their mother to make ornaments.

not an important element in the celebration of Christmas. Only after World War II did this custom begin to gain acceptance in the French home. Although the *crèche* goes up at the beginning of December, most families dress their tree just a few days before Christmas, so that it will stay fresh until the celebration of the Epiphany on January 6. Decorations tend to be simple, perhaps a few colored ornaments or ribbons and some small white lights.

EPIPHANY

Although Epiphany, or the arrival of the Three Kings, comes on January 6, the celebration of the holy day has expanded to embrace every Sunday in January. During that month, dessert for Sunday dinner is a cake called the *Galette des Rois*, the Cake of the Kings. This light, flaky pastry cake contains a small *fève*, or porcelain piece, traditionally in the shape of the Baby Jesus, but now often molded into the shapes of miniature animals and flowers. At the conclusion of the meal, one of the younger children is invited to hide underneath the table. Out of view, an adult cuts the cake one slice at a time and asks, "Who shall get this piece?" The child directs the serving of the pieces until everyone has received a slice. Whoever finds the little porcelain piece in his or her slice becomes king or queen of the day and receives a gold paper crown to wear for the rest of the afternoon. Walking around Paris in January it is a common sight to see young children proudly wearing golden paper crowns, evidence, perhaps, of a little parental gerrymandering.

THE KITCHEN

IT IS NO WONDER that the word that describes the art of cooking in France is the same word used to designate the room in which it is practiced: *la cuisine.* To the French, cooking and kitchen are indeed one and the same. And there are no secrets in the kitchen. In this room, the French want everything to be *sous la main,* or right at the fingertips, out in plain view. When they cook, the French want to see, at a glance, what they need, and then reach for it, without a moment's hesitation.

The kitchen is the heart of the French home and warmly reflects the personality of the homemaker. Stéphanie Deméry has a passion for collecting miniature stoves, which she displays in her kitchen.

To the unaccustomed, the French kitchen may appear to be cozy albeit cluttered, even disorganized. But the clutter is not disordered at all; in fact, there is a sublime organization inherent in the jumble that comes from the French penchant for layering and their delight in texture. Look at the clutter: earthenware jugs stuffed with wooden spoons and wire whisks, bowls overflowing with ripening fruit, a shelf laden with stacks of linen towels. From ceiling to floor, wherever the eye roams, something claims its space. Pots hang overhead, windowsills are fragrant with potted herbs, rows of clamp-capped Triomphe glass jars, filled with preserves, line the counters.

In some cases, most notably in city apartments, the cozy disorder may be attributed to a lack of space. Many buildings were constructed during an era when kitchens were the preserve of domestics and children, whose comfort and convenience did not command top priority. Although these attitudes are long gone, the physical restrictions of the kitchen remain, leaving little storage space and, by default, much left out in the open.

Lack of space alone, however, cannot fully explain the look of the French kitchen. Even in grand country houses where space is not limited, the art of cabinetry did not extend to kitchen storage, and open shelving or glass-paned cabinets are still the norm. The slick, ultramodern blueprint that conceals everything behind smooth, closed doors has few enthusiasts. Thus, the colorful, sometimes unruly stacks of plates, bowls, cups and glasses can continue to add to the visual texture of the kitchen.

A preference for natural materials characterizes the French kitchen: baskets woven of raffia, reed and straw; pottery and earthenwares; woods burnished by use, not wax; fruits and vegetables—and flowers. Finally, added to all this are the charmingly eccentric flea market "follies," such as a carved wooden pig or hand-painted cowbell, that are collected at whim and serve no discernible purpose save to provide pleasure.

Antique objects are right at home in the French kitchen, such as the wire basket at left, and the wooden butter mold above.

GETTING THE MOST FROM **STORAGE** SPACE

The French take enormous pride in their *astuces*, the ingenious little tricks that permit people to triumph over the challenges of daily life. In the kitchen, for the sake of efficiency and organization, many of these *astuces* take the form of inventive systems of stacking, hanging and storing. The French see the kitchen in terms of its cubic space, not just the linear space available on countertops and shelves. They use stacks of baskets and boxes, for example, to create cubbyholes and other nooks and crannies. A collection of old wine crates might be transformed into an impromptu wall unit. An assortment of metal hooks can be suspended from metal grids over the stove to hold pots, pans and other utensils. Hooks may also be screwed into a series of ceiling beams, or right into the ceiling itself, to hang braids of garlic or bunches of dried flowers or herbs.

Every inch of every cabinet is put to use. For example, because the trash can is the one object the French prefer to conceal, their version is small enough to affix to the inside of a cabinet below the sink. A clever pulley system lifts the lid when the cabinet door is opened and closes it again when the trash can tucks back in underneath the sink.

If sufficient space exists, hooks and clamps can be attached to organize brooms, dustpans and other necessaries.

Take full advantage of the opportunity to keep things close at hand. Consider mounting racks and shallow shelves in various configurations above work surfaces. Subdivide spaces to create small cubbies and make good use of multi-shelved rolling carts to keep things in reach.

Clutter is "lovable" when it is an eclectic assortment of natural materials like ceramic, wood and rattan.

Visual texture can be created in many ways: by hanging dried herbs or garlic ropes; grouping similarly shaped or colored glass bottles; and using unusual items, like wooden wine crates, to create open shelving. ABOVE: Sylvie Merten's solution for keeping baskets close at hand—suspending a chain from ceiling to floor and then hanging baskets from S-hooks —resulted in a marvelous focal point for the kitchen.

IF YOUR KITCHEN DOES NOT ALLOW FOR OVERHEAD RACKS FROM WHICH TO HANG POTS AND PANS, CONSIDER TRANSFORMING A CABINET INTO A HUTCH. SELECT AN ABOVE-COUNTER CABINET THAT HAS AT LEAST TWO AND A HALF FEET OF VERTICAL SPACE, REMOVE THE DOORS AND SHELVES AND ATTACH A METAL GRID TO THE CABINET'S INSIDE BACK WALL LARGE ENOUGH TO COVER THE ENTIRE VERTICAL SURFACE. THEN, USING METAL S-HOOKS, HANG YOUR POTS ON THE METAL GRID AND STACK EXTRAS ON THE BOTTOM SHELF. YOU WILL NOW HAVE BOTH EASY ACCESS TO YOUR COOKWARE AND THE VISUAL TEXTURE PROVIDED BY ITS VARIED SHAPES AND MATERIALS.

Wire racks and shelving can be a particularly good storage solution in the kitchen: they are lightweight, easily allow for the attachment of hooks, and, because they allow air to circulate freely, are practical in kitchens where pies, cakes and breads are baked often.

Colorful
Kitchen
Cottons

In country kitchens, a lively and inexpensive way to dress open cabinets and the sink is to skirt them with fabric. Most often, the fabric—usually a lightweight, colorful cotton in a bright Provençal miniprint, paisley or gingham —is gathered along a narrow rod affixed just under the countertop or sink. The material drops to within an inch or two of the floor and effectively conceals whatever is stored behind.

Another option for these fabrics is to place them behind glass-paneled doors. Two thin rods are mounted just above and beneath the glass and the fabric is gathered along them. Depending upon the volume of gathering desired, the amount of fabric used will be two to three times the width of the surface to be covered.

Charming lightweight cottons are a delightful and inexpensive way to bring country flavor to your kitchen. Behind the yellow chair, blue gingham is suspended from a thin rod to conceal storage space behind. RIGHT: A bright Souleiado print is gathered along thin rods mounted at top and bottom of the glass-paned door.

The Practical Beauty of **Tile**

The practical is no better married to the beautiful than on the tiled backsplashes and walls of French kitchens. With a wipe of the sponge all traces of even the most exuberant chef vanish. Virtually without exception, some portion of every kitchen is tiled. The range of tiles varies widely, from standard-issue high-gloss white squares that insulate the wall behind a stove in a small city apartment to the most delicately painted tiles rendered in faïence used to cover the entire wall surface of a kitchen in a grand country château. The tiles enliven the color palette in any kitchen and add design interest to the walls. They serve as a textural backdrop for utensils and foods, and they are also a good investment, since they last for generations.

There is no typically French approach to tiling kitchen walls. Tiles may be set on a diagonal grid, in a checkerboard config-uration or in a plain field outlined with a coordinating border in another hue. Because tile is rather costly, many families stretch their resources by purchasing a few lovely, expensive tiles—artisan crafted or antique, in many cases—and intersperse them strategically within an overall scheme.

Floor tiles are more conformist; most of these are laid out in grids using over-sized, glazed or unglazed terra-cotta squares or octagons filled with smaller squares at the corners.

Tiles add color and visual interest to a kitchen and are easily cleaned with a wipe of a sponge. If budget permits, consider investing in hand-decorated tiles, which can be interspersed with industrially produced tiles or arranged to cover an entire section of wall.

❖

THE

GLOW

OF

COPPER

Brittany is famous for its delicious paper-thin crêpes.
Equally memorable are the
enormous copper bowls in
which the batter is whisked,
and the pans in which the
crêpes are cooked and folded
before serving. They generate
a warm glow as soothing as
the sweet fragrances drifting
from the kitchen.

The French adore copper
both for its luster and for its
functional excellence. Of all
metals, it is the most efficient
conductor of heat and has
therefore long been the
choice of professional chefs.
Because of the chemistry
between copper and egg
whites, an unlined copper
bowl speeds the process of
whipping these into frothy
peaks. Copper also facilitates
the even cooking of soups
and sauces.

vent burning and ensure that the cooking progresses evenly.

"Copper has superior conductivity," Dulin continues, "and so the temperature of a pot, from bottom to top, remains uniform. In fact, if the bottom of a copper pot is one hundred degrees centigrade, the top will be only about two degrees cooler—there's virtually no loss of heat. The food cooks evenly and the chef doesn't have to stay glued to the pot."

The thickness of a copper pot should measure between 2.5 and 3.0 millimeters. Lesser-quality cookware, Dulin warns, will taper from the correct thickness at the top of the pot down to 1.0 or 1.5 millimeters. It may be very difficult to detect this deficiency with the naked eye, but a suspect pot will feel out of balance. When buying copper, if you seem to be getting a bargain too good to be true—you probably are.

At l'Atelier du Cuivre copperware is still crafted by hand. During the first stage—*le repoussage*—a flat copper disk is mounted on a machine and pressed into its desired shape by a mechanism designed to exert strong and even pressure on the metal (**1**).

The second stage is *l'étamage*, which describes the process of coating the inside of each piece with tin, known in France as *l'étain*.

When chefs speak of copper's superior conductivity, they are referring to the fact that, from top to bottom, a pan's temperature will be virtually uniform; thus foods cook evenly without constant stirring.

HOW COPPER IS MADE

In the picturesque little town of Villedieu-les-Poêles, about thirty minutes east of Mont Saint-Michel, artisans have been crafting copper for nine centuries. Etienne Dulin runs l'Atelier du Cuivre (the Copper Workshop) and invited me for a visit to learn more about his craft. When I asked Monsieur Dulin why copper retains such an outstanding reputation among professional cooks, in France and abroad, he explained, "In a way, copper is a labor-saving device. Because the temperature can vary as much as thirty degrees centigrade (about ninety degrees Fahrenheit) from the top to the bottom of a pot, a chef has to continually stir the contents to pre-

1

2

This is required by law for all copper used for cooking because as copper oxidizes, it produces a toxic substance. During *l'étamage,* the piece is first coated on the outside with a substance called *blanc d'Espagne* (literally, Spanish chalk) to prevent the tin from adhering to this surface (**2**). The piece is then heated over a flame to 230 degrees centigrade (450 degrees Fahrenheit). Molten tin is swirled inside the pot and fuses to the copper (**3**).

There are two exceptions to the requirement that copper cookware be coated with tin. The first is bowls, which are never used for cooking but only for whipping egg whites. The second is basins used in making jams. Sugar—a major component of jam—will stick to the tin lining when heated, making the basin impossible to clean.

Polishing, or *le polissage,* is the third step. A cotton-wrapped wheel spins at 1,500 revolutions per minute to bring up the rose-colored shine we associate with copper (**4**). This operation requires a steady hand; because of the speed of the wheel, the slightest error will wrench the piece from the polisher's hands.

Lastly the handles are attached. In French pieces, these handles are generally made of brass; heavyweight aluminum may also be used. When buying high-quality copper cookware, make sure the rivets do not break through the interior wall of the pot; this ensures a smooth surface that is stronger, easier to clean and aesthetically more pleasing.

Occasionally an additional step is introduced right after the copper is pressed into its desired shape. This is called *le martelage,* or hammering (**5**). Traditionally, the shaping of a piece was accomplished by hammering the copper disk or plate against a form, rather than by machine-pressing. Hammering actually increases the strength of copper; in fact connoisseurs of copper cookware look for signs of hammering, especially on the bottom of a piece where it takes the most wear and tear. Hammering is practiced today on basins for jams. It makes the interior of the basin perfectly round and smooth, thus preventing the sugar from adhering to any nooks or crannies during the cooking process.

A well-equipped French kitchen has a full range of copperwares: sauce and sauté pans, casseroles, basins for making jams and molds.

Copper is especially seductive for its decorative appeal. It is tempting to lacquer it to prevent discoloration, but this inhibits conductivity and should not be done. Polishing, however, adds patina, which enhances the look of copper and its value.

A superior quality copper pan will have a smooth interior surface with no rivets breaking through to the interior wall. This makes it stronger and easier to clean. When evaluating a copper pan, pick it up in your hand. It should feel well balanced.

PLEASURES
OF THE
TABLE

FOOD IS A source of enormous pleasure and pride in France. It is embraced as a top priority in daily life and accorded much thought, conversation and time. The average person has a seemingly encyclopedic knowledge of cheeses and wines as well as fiercely loyal ties to the specialties of his or her native region, be it foie gras from the southwest, *galettes* from Brittany or bouillabaisse from Marseilles.

Taking the time to find the freshest ingredients was a top priority for Noelle Girard, who prepared this beautiful terrine at her home in Provence.

It may take a little extra time to travel to the open-air market nearest you, but the quality and variety of the produce brought by area farmers will make your investment worthwhile.

Food Shopping with *SAVOIR-FAIRE*

The French have a contagiously upbeat attitude toward food marketing. Far from being viewed as a chore, it is looked upon as a form of entertainment. Neighbors compare notes on which vendors are offering the best merchandise on a given day; fathers take their children with them on Saturday excursions to select a treat for Sunday dinner; chance meetings between friends lead to rambling chats.

Spending an extra fifteen minutes to track down the ripest produce is considered worthwhile, especially when one considers the amount of time that will be spent enjoying the meal prepared from these ingredients.

To the French, marketing is simply the first in a series of steps leading up to a meal. When more care is taken in the selection of ingredients, more enjoyment is found in preparing them and even greater enjoyment will be felt in serving and eating the meal.

Going to the market is a sensuous affair, a time to smell, to touch, to listen, to examine. It is an adventure and a chance to excel at finding the perfect ingredient for the evening meal. The people who bring produce to open-air markets are very knowledgeable and can offer valuable information. Don't hesitate to ask for their help and advice.

HOW TO GET THE MOST OUT OF **MARKETING**

Follow the lead of the French when you go to the grocery store, specialty store or greenmarket. Do not hesitate to ask questions and request help. Not only will you become a more informed, involved shopper, you'll enjoy the experience more.

TALK TO MERCHANTS. People who work closely with their products are only too happy to share informa-  tion about their specialty. Ask the person behind the fish counter what he thinks is the best catch of the day, and how he would prepare it. Does he have a special recipe he would share? Talk to the person selling cheese. (The French are extremely precise about expressing their needs when purchasing a cheese; they specify the time they want to serve the cheese and trust their merchant to select the proper piece for them.) Describe the flavor you prefer, and ask if there is anything you might try.

ASK FOR A SAMPLE. Many markets have discovered that it is good business to offer samples to their customers. You are much more likely to buy a new prod-uct if you have a chance to taste it first. So take advantage of the opportunity to sample: you may discover a great new taste you would have otherwise passed up.

USE YOUR SENSE OF SMELL. Good food smells good. It may take a little practice, but you should be able to select the right melon, the right peach, the right berries and so forth simply by the sweetness of their fragrance. In the United States, food is often cultivated for appearance; the most beautiful produce, however, is not necessarily the best tasting. Your sense of smell matters most when buying fish. Fresh fish has no odor at all. The fish merchant should let you smell a piece of fish before you purchase.

LEARN HOW TO BUY. The French are accustomed to shopping every day, but even if you don't have time to go to the greenmarket that often, you don't have to give up the bounty of fresh produce. Some fruits and vegetables, for instance, keep longer than others, so plan your weekly menus accordingly. Eat perishables such as fresh corn or ripe berries first. At midweek, prepare zucchini or yellow squash or tomatoes, which have a longer shelf life. Save the hardiest vegetables and fruits for the end of the week; root vegetables such as carrots or potatoes and fruits such as apples or pears will definitely last a week.

While marketing in France, I learned not only to specify the type of cheese I wanted, but also when I wanted to serve it.

⚜

MUSINGS ABOUT SIMPLE FOODS

"I don't think French cuisine is complicated at all," asserts jewelry designer Carole Rochas, known for her delicious dinner parties. "It's simply a question of mastering *les petites bases*, the little building blocks." She gives as an example her method of making a sauce for a roast. When braising the roast, take a moment or two to dice some onions, a tomato, carrots and celery, and toss them into the same pan. When the roast is done, remove it to a platter and skim the fat from the pan. Add a little white wine and water to the juices and scrape the delicious morsels from the bottom of the pan gently while stirring and reheating. *Voilà!* A perfect sauce.

It is also a myth that all French cuisine is time-consuming. In the Rochas household, a favorite dish is calamari sautéed and served with potatoes. "I first quickly slice the calamari—not too thick, not too thin. Then I heat some butter and olive oil in a pan, add a couple of cloves of pressed garlic, some sprigs of Italian parsley, and sauté these with the calamari for five minutes. To speed up the cooking of the potatoes, I heat them through in the microwave, then chop them coarsely and sauté them for five minutes in the olive oil. It's heavenly!"

Martha Rose Schulman is an American who spent twelve years living in France researching and writing cookbooks on the cuisine of Provence and the Mediterranean Coast. When asked how her time in France affected her cooking techniques, she responds instantly, "It's lightened my touch." Lightened? With all the rich creams and butters used in French cuisine? "Yes," she exclaims, "the French are purists when it comes to honoring their ingredients. Their dishes are neither complicated nor busy." Only a few high-quality ingredients are selected to make many of their finest dishes: chicken roasted with garlic, for example, or potatoes baked with fennel, or fish poached in white wine and seasoned with fresh herbs.

For photographer Arnaud de Wildenberg, the joy of cooking is related not only to simple ingredients but also to fresh ones. "I love to spend the day out on my boat fishing for sea bass with my friends. Then we roast the bass we have just caught in the fireplace." De Wildenberg rubs the fish with some oil, adds salt and pepper to taste and accompanies the just-caught bass with some new red potatoes, wrapped in foil and baked alongside. All that remains is to pour the wine and wish *bon appetit!*

Photographer Arnaud de Wildenberg knows there is no better way to insure the fish is fresh than to go out and catch it yourself.

If It's November, This Must Be ROQUEFORT

France takes its cheese very seriously. Volumes are written on how to care for cheese, how to cut into it, how to present it and what it should accompany. Most French cheese is unpasteurized, and since nonpasteurized milk has a seasonality depending on the grazing habits of the animal, different cheeses even have different seasons. It could take years to learn about every variety of cheese produced in France. Much less daunting is to become familiar with the half-dozen superstars.

Cheese Quandaries

Is the crust of cheeses such as Brie and chèvre edible? MANY OF THE FRENCH WILL EAT THE SOFT, SNOWY-WHITE CRUSTS THAT SURROUND THEIR FAVORITE CHEESES. BECAUSE THIS IS AN ACQUIRED TASTE, YOU MAY PREFER TO CUT AWAY THE CRUST FIRST.

Is there a way to prevent a creamy cheese from clinging to the knife? BRUSH A THIN LAYER OF PEANUT OR ALMOND OIL ON THE KNIFE.

How many cheeses are normally served for a cheese course? TRADITIONALLY THREE OR SOMETIMES FIVE WERE OFFERED. TODAY THERE IS A TREND TOWARD SERVING JUST ONE FAVORITE CHEESE, OR SEVERAL VARIETIES OF THE SAME CHEESE, SUCH AS BRIE DE MEAUX FERMIER, BRIE LAITIER AND BRIE DE MELUN.

What kind of a platter should be used to serve cheese? THE SIMPLER THE BETTER. THE PLATTER SHOULD BE LARGE ENOUGH SO THAT THE CHEESES DO NOT TOUCH. IF YOU ARE SERVING A STRONG CHEESE, SUCH AS ROQUEFORT, WITH A MILDER CHEESE, PROVIDE A SEPARATE KNIFE FOR EACH.

CHÈVRE
Made from: Goat's milk.
Percentage of Fat: 45%.
General Characteristics: Chèvre is a thick, dry, slightly crumbly and tangy cheese. The crust can range from snowy white to golden in hue, although the cheese itself is white. Chèvre comes in many shapes, including "buttons," larger rounds, cylindrical sticks, and pyramids. It will vary in odor from a light goat-milk odor to a more penetrating one.
How to Serve: Buttons are cut in half; rounds are cut into wedges; cylinders are sliced in small rounds; pyramids are sliced into wedges from the center down to the base.

ROQUEFORT
Made from: Sheep's milk.
Percentage of Fat: 45 - 50%.
General Characteristics: Roquefort is a strong blue cheese with a buttery consistency. Because it has no crust, it is wrapped in foil. It is made in large rounds that appear cylindrical, and is sold by the wedge. Roquefort has a very particular and penetrating odor, somewhat mildewlike.
How to Serve: Lay the wedge on its side. Slice from the center point of the thin edge toward the outer borders.

CAMEMBERT

Made from: Cow's milk.

Percentage of Fat: 45 - 50%.

General Characteristics:

Camembert is a creamy, supple, slightly pungent cheese, with an ivory cast. Made in rounds, it is generally packaged in thin wooden boxes. (A French shopper will not hesitate to open the box and push her thumb into the round to check for ripeness; a perfectly ripe Camembert will spring back slowly to shape.) Camembert has an earthy odor.

How to Serve: Cut in wedges and allow to soften.

PONT-L'ÉVÊQUE

Made from: Cow's milk.

Percentage of Fat: 50%.

General Characteristics: Pont-l'Évêque is a soft, somewhat runny, strong-tasting cheese. Its crust is lightly striated with fine golden-yellow lines. It is made in squares. Pont-l'Évêque has a well-developed earthy odor.

How to Serve: Although it might seem more logical to cut rectangular pieces from the square, the cheese is cut in wedges, starting from the center then going out.

REBLOCHON

Made from: Cow's milk.

Percentage of Fat: 45 - 50%.

General Characteristics: Reblochon is a creamy, supple cheese with a rosy orange crust covered in a fine white powder. The cheese itself is a soft ivory. It is sometimes sold in two versions, one slightly more mild, or *plus doux,* than the other. Although made in rounds, it is often sold by the half round. Reblochon has a slight earthy odor.

How to Serve: Cut in wedges.

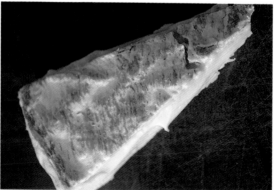

BRIE

Made from: Cow's milk.

Percentage of Fat: 45%.

General Characteristics: Brie is a soft, mild cheese, often infused with herbs. Although it is made in large rounds, it is generally sold in wedges. Look for a downy white crust and a soft creamy color. The cheese should feel soft and supple, and as it ripens, will begin to swell out from under the skin along the cut edges. Brie has a soft, earthy, even slightly musty odor.

How to Serve: Let soften and cut in long slices.

WINE: ALL YOU NEED ARE THE BASICS

The French love wine and serve it with dinner as a matter of course. A glass of wine is also typically taken with lunch as well. Because they grow up with wine at the table, the French trust their instincts—and their biases—and are not afraid to experiment with something new. Although the taste for wine continues to grow in the United States, many Americans still feel a bit intimidated by the range and selection of wines offered in the wineshop, and wonder which wines to serve with what. But wine buying should all come down to a very simple premise: Drink what you enjoy. For this, an encyclopedic knowledge of wine is not necessary.

If you would like a working acquaintanceship with French wines, you need only master a minimum level in label-reading skills. Fortunately, the French have already taken a great deal of the guesswork out of judging wines by classifying them and ranking them according to their quality.

The simplest wines—*ordinaires*, or ordinary table wines—are called *Vins de Pays*. This category was established just twenty years ago to recognize the amiability of simple local wines that had no pretense to greatness.

The next rank of wines are those that still are usually drunk locally. Called *Vins Délimités de Qualité Supérieure* (and coded VDQS), these wines are markedly superior to the *ordinaires* in terms of quality.

The highest classification embraces the so-called AOC wines. These *Vins d'Appellation d'Origine Contrôlée* are rigorously judged and strictly controlled according to a number of variables. The majority of French wines imported to the United States fall into this category, assuring Americans of a quality wine. AOC wines, of course, tend to be more expensive, but there are good buys, too.

Another designation to look for is the word *cru*. This refers to the "growth" of the grapes and their quality. In its simplest form, *grand cru* is the highest marking and *premier cru* is the next best. Lesser wines are not allowed to carry the *cru* distinction. Thus, if you see

Encyclopedic knowledge of wine is unnecessary. Just learn a few label-reading skills, then drink what you enjoy.

an AOC *grand cru* wine at a good price, buy it. It's worth the risk.

Wines may also be labeled as to whether they are *mise en bouteille au château*, or bottled in the producer's own cellars. The year the wine was bottled, or vintage, is also indicated. As a general rule, the more specific the label, the better the wine.

Although France produces hundreds of wines, most of the finer vineyards are concentrated within five wine regions: Bordeaux, Burgundy, Champagne, the Loire Valley and the Rhone Valley.

The WINE Regions

BORDEAUX

Bordeaux wines are recognized by their tall, upright bottles with straight shoulders. Many of the most complex and finest red wines of France come from this region; the area grows an equal number of whites, but these do not have the same reputation. Bordeaux reds should not be drunk "young"; they should be "laid down" for a number of years. Consult a vintage chart or a reputable wine merchant before choosing a particular year. Bordeaux wines are classified first by the area in which the grapes are grown, then more specifically by the district, even more specifically by the parish and finally, most specifically, by the actual producer, often a château. Thus an *Appellation Bordeaux Contrôlée* would be a fine wine; an *Appellation Médoc Contrôlée* (a district within Bordeaux) even better; an *Appellation Pauillac Contrôlée* (a parish within the district of Médoc) better still; and an *Appellation Château-Rothschild* (a château within the parish of Pauillac) would be an excellent wine.

The regional names belonging to Bordeaux are:

Médoc and Haut-Médoc	*Classic reds*
Margaux	*Delicate, refined reds*
Saint-Julien	*Gentle reds*
Pauillac	*Smooth, rich reds*
Graves	*Pale whites and some reds*
Sauternes	*Sweet whites*
Saint-Emilion	*Fine, rich reds*
Pomerol	*Deep, gentle reds*
Entre-Deux-Mers	*Light, fruity whites*

BURGUNDY

Burgundy is so large and diverse an area that reading a label and making a selection from among its offerings can be quite confusing. Compared to Bordeaux, for example, Burgundy has many more *appellations* (over 100 AOCs) and more growers sharing an *appellation*. You will sometimes see the name Bourgogne on the label, which is essentially meaningless; it indicates that a certain type of grape was used and does not designate a specific region. However, since the soil varies so much from area to area, the same type of grape will taste different depending on its actual origins.

Burgundy wines are recognized by their rounder bottles with gently sloping shoulders. Some of the more recognizable regional names belonging to Burgundy are:

Chablis*	*Light, dry whites*
Côte de Beaune	*Refined reds and renowned whites*
Volnay	*Smooth, fragrant reds*
Meursault	*Soft, dry whites*
Puligny-Montrachet	*Dry, slightly fruity whites*
Beaujolais	*Light, fruity, drinkable reds, lower in alcohol; drink young*
Saint-Véran	*Delicate whites*
Pouilly-Fuissé	*Pale, delicate whites*

*Chablis has been afflicted with a widespread cavalier misappropriation of its name; it is the world's most imitated white wine, especially among makers of jug wines.

TO PREVENT A SENSE OF BEING OVERWHELMED BY INFORMATION, CONSIDER FOCUSING ON ONLY ONE WINE REGION AT A TIME, FOR EXAMPLE, BORDEAUX. EXPERIMENT WITH THE DIFFERENT *APPELLATIONS* WITHIN BORDEAUX AND WAIT UNTIL YOU ARE COMFORTABLE SELECTING A FEW FAVORITES BEFORE MOVING ON TO THE NEXT WINE REGION.

CHAMPAGNE

Champagne is not, strictly speaking, a table wine. Champagne is a district northeast of Paris that has concentrated its wine-making efforts on the manufacture of the sparkling wine that has taken its name. The *méthode champenoise*, which is a secondary fermentation of still wine, comprises a series of rigorously controlled steps that result in what we call Champagne.

The only sparkling wines that are legally allowed to be called Champagne are those that come from this region and adhere to the restrictions. Thus there is no *appellation controlée* marking: the word "Champagne" is your assurance of quality. Two other major differences exist between Champagne and still wine: the vast majority of Champagnes do not indicate a vintage year and they are sold under a brand name, such as Perrier-Jouët, rather than a vineyard name. The exception to the vintage marking is those rare years when a particularly good crop is harvested. Vintage Champagnes are richer, more complex—and more expensive.

The stratification of Champagnes is based on how sweet they are. The sweetness comes from the amount of sugar added (the *dosage*) before the final corking:

Extra Brut	*No sugar added, very dry*
Brut	*Dry*
Extra Sec	*Slightly sweet*
Sec	*More sweet*
Demi-Sec	*Sweet*
Doux	*Very sweet*

The word *cuvée* refers to the contents of a *cuve*, or vat. Sometimes Champagne makers will identify a particularly fine wine with the terms *"cuvée spéciale"* or *"grande cuvée."*

A great French Champagne can easily run to more than $100 a bottle. But a very good Champagne can be purchased for between $25 to $35. Some choices in this range are:

Piper-Heidsieck
Mumm's Cordon Rouge
Veuve Clicquot
Moët et Chandon White Star
Taittinger
Perrier-Jouët

LOIRE VALLEY

The Loire, extending 600 miles inland from the Atlantic, is the longest river in France and therefore defines a very big wine region. Although a good variety of wines come from this region, it is probably most famous for its whites, which are crisp, dry and generally very good values. The generic whites of the area are known as "Anjou" wines, although some Anjou wines are, in fact, pink or red. The regional names belonging to the Loire are:

Muscadet	*Dry, light whites that are inexpensive*
Touraine	*Light, easy whites, a less costly alternative to the Sancerres*
Vouvray	*Can vary from dry to sweet whites*
Pouilly-Fumé	*Very fine whites*
Pouilly-sur-Loire	*Light dry whites, good alternative to Pouilly-Fumé at slightly lower cost*
Sancerre	*Very good whites; flinty, slightly spicy*

WINE ETIQUETTE AND PLEASURE

• THE HOST OR *MAÎTRE DE MAISON* ASSUMES RESPONSIBILITY FOR THE WINE.

• THE HOST TASTES THE WINE BEFORE SERVING IT TO ANY GUESTS. THIS AVOIDS PUTTING A GUEST IN THE UNCOMFORTABLE POSITION OF DEALING WITH A BAD WINE. AFTER MAKING SURE THE WINE IS GOOD, THE HOST SERVES EACH OF HIS GUESTS IN TURN — FIRST THE WOMEN, THEN THE MEN.

• GLASSES ARE FILLED TO THE HALFWAY POINT, NO MORE.

• BEFORE TASTING THE WINE, EVERYONE, HOST AND GUESTS, TAKES THE TIME TO APPRECIATE ITS BOUQUET.

• THE HOST KEEPS A CAREFUL EYE ON EVERYONE'S WINEGLASS, MAKING SURE THEY REMAIN HALF FULL.

• IF THE TABLE IS TOO LARGE FOR THE HOST TO COMFORTABLY REACH EVERYONE'S GLASS, HE WILL INVITE ONE OR MORE OF HIS MALE GUESTS TO WATCH THE GLASSES OF THE WOMEN TO HIS RIGHT AND LEFT, AS WELL AS HIS OWN. WOMEN TRADITIONALLY NEVER TOUCH THE WINE BOTTLE.

RHONE VALLEY

Rhone wines are named after the river that runs through the valley where they are produced. This area is famous for its red wines, which account for more than 90 percent of the production. Most of the wines from this valley are blended, and thus are sold by a cooperative rather than a single vineyard or commune. A *Côte du Rhône appellation* means that the wines come from the north of the region, while *Côtes du Rhône-Villages* means they come from the south. If you see only these marks on the label, with no accompanying château or winery, it may mean the wine is of somewhat lesser quality. Since these bottles will be much lower in price, however, they may be worth giving a try. The regional names belonging to the Rhone are:

Châteauneuf-du-Pape	*Dark, rich, deep reds*
Hermitage	*Dark, portlike reds*
Côte-Rotie	*Complex, rich reds*

READING A LABEL

THE NAME OF THE WINE

THE *APPELLATION* (Régnié is a type of Beaujolais wine)

CONCLUSION: Since it is a Beaujolais, this is a light, fruity red meant to be drunk young.

THE NAME AND ADDRESS OF THE COMPANY THAT BOTTLES THE WINE. Note that it is not "mise en bouteille au château" even though the name is "Château des Vergers."

A LA FRANÇAISE

✦

SIMPLE
PLEASURES

In perfect symmetry with the sophisticated culinary masterworks that France is famous for are the country's plain, unpretentious dishes of extraordinary quality. Even a simple sandwich is impeccably made. A sandwich of *jambon-beurre*, made with ham and butter, may be the low-priced mainstay of the café menu, but the bread is a fresh-baked baguette, the butter is creamy and sweet, and the ham is perfectly fresh and thinly sliced.

HOW TO MAKE A SANDWICH

Ingredients: A narrow baguette; sweet butter; best-quality ham from the butcher or deli, sliced thin; camembert or another cheese, if desired

WITH A SERRATED KNIFE, SPLIT THE BAGUETTE LENGTHWISE.

GENEROUSLY BUTTER EACH HALF.

PLACE TWO OR THREE SLICES OF HAM ON ONE HALF.

IF DESIRED, PLACE THREE OR FOUR SLICES OF CHEESE ON THE OTHER.

POUR A SMALL GLASS OF RED OR ROSÉ TABLE WINE.

RELAX.

How to Drink Coffee

Drinking coffee is a ritual act in France. Small hits of extra-strong coffee laced with sugar are considered appropriate at any time of the day. *Café au lait* or coffee with milk (also known as *café crème*) is strictly a pre-noon affair. The "morning cup" is actually more often a small bowl, with or without a handle. The milk is steamed and mixed with the coffee in equal parts; if the bowl is large, it is raised to the lips with both hands. Take-out coffee in paper cups is considered undesirable, if not completely uncivilized. Instead, when the need for a coffee arises, one simply leaves the office for a quick break at the nearest café.

ALTHOUGH THE FRENCH ARE NOT OVERLY CONCERNED WITH CHOLESTEROL, THEY RARELY INDULGE IN HEAVY MEALS. THEY SIP A *CAFÉ AU LAIT* BEFORE HEADING OUT TO WORK AND GENERALLY ESCHEW FOOD BEFORE LUNCH. EGGS, WHICH AMERICANS TEND TO ASSOCIATE WITH BREAKFAST, ARE INSTEAD WORKED INTO MANY CLASSIC AND POPULAR DISHES EATEN AT LUNCH OR FOR SUPPER. HEARTY SALADS WILL SOMETIMES INCLUDE A FRIED EGG AND, OF COURSE, THE HARD-BOILED EGG IS A CRITICAL ELEMENT OF A *SALADE NIÇOISE.*

Oeuf à la Coque

How to Eat an Egg

Oeuf à la Coque

Sunday dinner, served in the early afternoon, is the most ample meal of the week. Thus, the French often simply soft-boil an egg for a light Sunday supper. The egg is accompanied by mouillettes, slender slivers of toasted, buttered bread, and a light red wine.

Boil a very fresh egg for 3 to 4 minutes in water to which a pinch of salt and a drop or two of vinegar have been added.

Remove the egg from the water and place it in an egg cup. Put the wider part of the egg facing up because there is a little pocket of air at that end which makes it easier to cut into. Let it rest.

To prepare the *mouillettes,* toast slabs of country bread, or heat a baguette. When toasted, cut into spears about 4 to 6 inches long. Butter the *mouillettes.*

Using a spoon, tap around a small circle on top of the egg to break the shell. Lift off the cap to reveal the yolk. Using *mouillettes,* dip into the egg yolk and enjoy! Finish off remainder of egg with a spoon if necessary.

Oeuf Mimosa

This dish, which takes its name from its resemblance to the color of the mimosa flower, makes a nice light lunch or supper. It is served at room temperature. It can be accompanied by a light red or rosé wine.

Boil an egg for 10 minutes until hard-boiled. Remove it from the water and let cool slightly.

Remove from shell.

With a fork, mash the egg coarsely. Slice a cucumber as thinly as possible and arrange slices in a spiral from the outside edge of a plate toward its center, overlapping them.

Spoon the mashed egg over the cucumber slices. Garnish with a sprig of mint.

Add salt and pepper to taste; add a pinch of paprika for color.

Oeuf Mayonnaise

This is another egg dish that makes a nice light lunch or supper, and once again it can be accompanied by a light red or rosé wine.

Boil an egg, as above, for 10 minutes. Remove it from the water, cool slightly and remove it from the shell.

Cut the egg in half lengthwise. Spoon out the yolk into a small bowl.

Mash the yolk with 1 tablespoon of mayonnaise, preferably homemade, until smooth.

Refill the egg halves. Add salt and pepper to taste, paprika for color.

Serve with buttered toast.

Oeufs Brouillés

(for two)

Scrambled eggs are a standby in the French home; their version is stirred gently, without the addition of milk. For a single serving, use two large eggs instead of the four called for here.

Using a fork, whip together four eggs in a large bowl with salt and pepper to taste and a pinch of nutmeg.

Toast two thick slabs of country bread, and set each upon a plate.

Over a medium flame, melt a pat of butter in a nonstick skillet. When the butter is melted and bubbly, but not brown, pour in the egg mixture all at once. Stir constantly until the eggs hold together; do not let them dry out.

Turn the eggs onto the toasted bread. Sprinkle chopped herbs, such as fines herbes or parsley, on top to taste.

Oeuf Mimosa

Oeuf Mayonnaise

Oeufs Brouillés

CLASSIC FRENCH MEALS

✦

MENU 1 *
(SERVES FOUR)

GRUYÈRE SOUFFLÉ

VEAL FORESTIER WITH SPINACH

MIXED GREEN SALAD

CHEESE PLATTER

MELONS FILLED WITH BERRIES

GRUYÈRE SOUFFLÉ

3 eggs, beaten
6 tablespoons flour
1 can (300 ml) unsweetened
    evaporated milk
Salt and pepper to taste
½ cup Gruyère, grated

Preheat oven to 375°.
    Beat together eggs, flour and milk, adding salt and pepper to taste.
    Pour the mixture into an oiled medium baking dish with sides at least 2" high.
    Sprinkle the grated Gruyère cheese on top.
    Place in oven for 20 to 25 minutes, or until the soufflé has puffed up and is nicely golden. Serve immediately.

VEAL FORESTIER

3 tablespoons butter
Salt and pepper to taste, and
    any other favorite seasonings
4 veal cutlets
1 cup mushrooms (use what is best
    at market)
½ cup heavy cream
1 egg yolk

Melt 2 tablespoons of the butter in a nonstick frying pan.
    Season and sauté the veal, 3 to 4 minutes on each side, depending upon thickness of cutlet.
    While veal is cooking, clean the mushrooms. Put the other tablespoon of butter into a small saucepan and sauté the mushrooms until they soften and release their juice. Set aside and keep warm.
    When the veal is sautéed to your liking, remove from heat and place on a platter, reserving pan juices. Surround the veal with spinach (recipe follows).
    Allow the frying pan to cool for a minute. (If it is too hot you will scald the cream and overcook the egg yolk.) Add the cream and the egg yolk to the pan and stir in the juices from the veal. Add mushrooms and stir to blend. Pour finished sauce over the veal.

SPINACH

1 pound fresh spinach leaves,
    washed and trimmed, or two packages (10 oz.) frozen chopped
    spinach, prepared according to
    package directions
1 tablespoon fresh lemon juice

If preparing fresh spinach, bring a small amount of salted water (about ¼" on bottom of pan) to a boil. Cook for 2 to 3 minutes or until leaves have wilted. Drain, then stir in lemon juice. If using frozen spinach, add lemon juice after it is prepared.
    Arrange cooked spinach on platter surrounding the veal cutlets.

This meal is pictured on pages 116 and 117.

MIXED GREEN SALAD

Salad greens
1 hard-boiled egg, chopped

Wash and drain a mixture of your favorite salad greens and place in salad bowl. Toss with vinaigrette (recipe follows).

Sprinkle the chopped egg in a line across the top of the salad.

VINAIGRETTE

Zest and juice of ½ lemon
¼ cup extra virgin olive oil
1 teaspoon Dijon mustard
1 garlic clove, finely minced
2 tablespoons red wine vinegar
½ teaspoon sugar
Salt and pepper to taste

Whisk together all the ingredients and toss with the salad. You may want to experiment with the quantities of the ingredients until you find the combination that most pleases you.

CHEESE PLATTER

Serve an assortment of 3 to 5 of your favorite cheeses. Offer a range of cheeses from mild to strong. Serve with good, crusty French bread.

MELONS FILLED WITH BERRIES

2 ripe cantaloupes
1 to 2 cups mixed raspberries, strawberries and any other red berries
Vanilla Sugar (recipe follows)

Cut melons in half. Remove seeds, then scoop out fruit and cube into one-inch chunks.

Mix cubes with fresh red berries and place the fruit mixture back into the melon halves.

Sprinkle with vanilla sugar.

VANILLA SUGAR

Leave 2 sticks of vanilla in a 1-pound container of white granulated sugar for a week or two. The sugar will take on a vanilla flavor.

MENU 2
(SERVES FOUR)

ARTICHAUTS DE FLORENCE

ROASTED CHICKEN WITH GARLIC

MASHED POTATOES WITH CELERY ROOT

MIXED GREEN SALAD

CHEESE PLATTER

TARTE TATIN

ARTICHAUTS DE FLORENCE

This dish is named after Florence Jonchères, who gave me the recipe after serving these delicious artichoke entrées at a dinner party in her home in Paris.

8 artichoke bottoms, precooked or fresh
Juice from ½ lemon
½ cup blue cheese (such as Roquefort or Gorgonzola)
½ cup crème fraîche
½ cup shelled walnuts, broken into small pieces
Salt and pepper to taste

Preheat oven to 350°.

If using precooked artichoke bottoms, which can be found in the deli or charcuterie sections of specialty food stores, place a few drops of lemon juice in each, then reheat in the oven for about 5 minutes. (Time will vary according to your oven.) They should still be firm.

If you are using fresh artichokes, cut the stems and tops off 8 globe artichokes. Next, break off leaves and cut away any tough skin from the bottom. As you prepare each artichoke dip it in lemon juice so it won't discolor. Simmer in salted water for 30 minutes, or until tender. Remove the hairy choke from the center with a spoon.

While the artichokes are cooking, mix together the blue cheese, crème fraîche and walnut pieces. Season to taste.

Fill each artichoke bottom with a spoonful of the cheese mixture.

Place them on a cookie sheet and bake in oven for about 10 minutes, or until the tops are golden.

Allow the artichokes to cool until just warm.

Place 2 stuffed artichokes on each plate; garnish with a few red and green lettuce leaves dressed in vinaigrette.

ROASTED CHICKEN WITH GARLIC

1 3- to 4-pound roasting chicken
10 to 12 cloves garlic, peeled
¼ teaspoon dried thyme, or 1 to 2
  tablespoons chopped fresh thyme
¼ teaspoon dried rosemary, or 1 to 2
  tablespoons chopped fresh rosemary
Salt and pepper to taste
2 tablespoons softened butter, plus
  extra for basting

Preheat oven to 400°.

Using a small knife to pierce the skin of the chicken, insert the peeled garlic cloves, distributing them evenly over the breast and thighs.

Mix the herbs, salt and pepper into the butter.

Rub the chicken inside and out with the butter and herb mixture.

Place the chicken on a rack in a roasting pan.

Roast the chicken uncovered, basting occasionally with additional melted butter. Depending upon your oven and the size of the bird, it will take about an hour to an hour and a half. (Pierce the chicken with a knife; if juices run clear it should be done.) Let it stand for a few minutes before carving.

MASHED POTATOES WITH CELERY ROOT

4 large red potatoes
1 celery root
¼ to ½ cup milk
Salt and pepper to taste

Peel and cube potatoes and celery root. Boil in a large pot of salted water until tender, about 10 to 15 minutes; drain thoroughly.

Using a hand mixer, beat in milk until you reach desired consistency. Add salt and pepper. (If you like, add a small amount of butter.)

CHEESE PLATTER

As a simpler alternative to serving a selection of different cheeses, try serving just one special and very delicious cheese. Don't forget the French bread.

TARTE TATIN

1 cup all-purpose flour
¼ teaspoon salt
8 tablespoons unsalted butter
¼ cup plus one tablespoon ice water
4 large apples
½ cup sugar

In a food processor, pulse flour, salt and 4 tablespoons of butter together until mixture starts to hold together. Add ice water slowly until a ball of dough begins to form. Wrap the dough in plastic and refrigerate for at least half an hour.

Peel the apples and cut into thick slices.

Melt the remaining 4 tablespoons of butter and pour into a 9-inch oven-proof skillet or *génoise* pan. Sprinkle half the sugar on top.

Arrange the apple pieces to cover bottom of pan. (They should be packed tightly.) Sprinkle remaining sugar on top of apples.

Place the pan on the stove over high heat for about 20 minutes, or until the sugar carmelizes to a light brown.

Preheat oven to 350°.

Roll the dough into a thin crust. Cover the pan containing the apples with the crust, tucking the edges down into the pan.

Bake in oven for 30 minutes.

Invert the tarte onto a serving plate and let cool to room temperature before serving.

RESOURCES

WHERE TO BUY PRODUCTS SHOWN IN THIS BOOK

Many wonderful French products for the home are available in the United States. Large department stores such as Bloomingdale's, Neiman-Marcus, Bergdorf-Goodman, and Saks Fifth Avenue are good resources, as are the many French specialty food and home furnishings stores found in most large cities.

Below is a list of retailers in the United States who carry many of the fabrics and the specific items shown for the table. Telephone and fax numbers of companies in France are also provided, should you wish to contact a company directly. (Note: When calling or faxing France from the United States, you must dial 011-33. If you are phoning Paris, you must also dial 1 before the eight-digit number.)

PRODUCT INFORMATION FROM HOW TO SET A TABLE

Page 98: Dinner plate and charger from the Laure Japy Collection. Quilted tablecloth from Souleiado. Glassware from Casa Lopez.

Page 99, clockwise from top: Yellow tablecloth and blue underskirt from Christian Dior. Oiseau Blue dinner plate from Porcelaine de Paris. Crochet-trimmed tablecloth from Siècle, linen underskirt from Muriel Grateau. Silver by Christian Dior. Chan Kai dinner plate from Puiforcat, charger from Laure Japy.

Page 101, top to bottom: Tablecloth from Souleiado. Tarascon dinner plate from Souleiado. La Chasse dinner plate from Hermès.

Page 102, top to bottom: Les Marquises dinner collection from Souleiado. Saint Cloud dinner collection from Bernardaud.

Page 105, Collection Marie-Antoinette from Bernardaud.

TABLE/BED LINENS

Handblock
(Tablecloth shown on page 121 is Louisiana in the color Wine)
487 Columbus Avenue
New York, NY 10024
212-799-4342
212-873-4401 (fax)

860 Lexington Avenue
New York, NY 10021
212-570-1816
212-570-9587 (fax)

Souleiado
(Fabrics shown on page 33, tablecloths on pages 98, 100–101)
Museum/shop open to public:
39, rue Proudhon
13150 Tarascon, France
90-91-08-80
90-91-17-60 (fax)

P.O. Box 150
53 Main Street
Bar Harbor, ME 04609
207-288-2828
207-288-9890 (fax)

83 Greenwich Avenue
Greenwich, CT 06830
203-862-9133

Souleiado fabrics also available at:
Pierre Deux Boutique
404 Irvington Street
Pleasantville, NY 10570
914-747-4111
914-747-4291 (fax)
Call for information on boutiques in Atlanta, Boston, Carmel, Dallas, New York, Palm Beach, San Francisco and Winnetka.

Country Loft Antiques
88 Main Street North
Woodbury, CT 06798
203-266-4500
203-266-4502 (fax)

Christian Dior
(Blue and yellow tablecloth on page 99)
11, rue François 1er
75008 Paris
40-73-54-44
47-20-00-60 (fax)

Muriel Grateau
(Tablecloth shown on page 99)
Studio 29
29-31, rue de Valois
75001 Paris
40-20-90-30
42-96-12-32 (fax)

Siècle
(Crochet-trimmed tablecloth on page 99)
24, rue du Bac
75007 Paris
47-03-48-03, 47-03-48-02
47-03-48-01 (fax)

Yves Halard*
(Table linens/porcelains shown on page 93)
252 Bis, Blvd St. Germain
75007 Paris
42-22-60-50
45-48-86-93 (fax)

*Michèle Halard also designs tableware, linens, glassware and furniture for other French manufacturers including Laurer, Ateliers du Vivarais, Royal Limoges and Plasait. Inquiries can be made via fax.

Porthault
18 East 69 Street
New York, NY 10021
212-688-1660
212-772-8450 (fax)

PORCELAIN

Bernardaud Limoge
(Shown on pages 102, 105)
11, rue Royale
75008 Paris
47-42-82-66, 47-42-61-51
49-24-06-35, 47-42-60-06 (fax)

777 Madison Avenue
New York, NY 10021
800-884-7775, 212-737-7775
212-794-9730 (fax)

Hermès
(Shown on page 101)
24, rue du Faubourg St. Honoré
75008 Paris
40-17-47-17
40-17-48-73, 40-17-47-18 (fax)

11 East 57 Street
New York, NY 10022
800-441-4488, 212-751-3181
212-751-7143 (fax)

Porcelaine de Paris
(Shown on pages 99, 106–107)
8, rue de la Pierre-Levée
75543 Paris Cedex 11
43-57-40-35
43-57-99-80 (fax)

Showroom:
13, rue de Pierre Levy
75011 Paris
49-29-99-20
Monday–Saturday 10 a.m.–6 p.m.

In the United States, call:
The Blachere Group
41 Madison Avenue, Suite 22C
New York, NY 10010
212-683-4936, 914-779-3787
914-337-6317 (fax)

Laure Japy
(Shown on page 98)
123, rue Léopold Rechossière
93300 Aubervilliers, France
(1) 48-33-86-33
(1) 48-33-48-93 (fax)
Laure Japy is also available in Bloomingdale's

Puiforcat
(Shown on page 99)
811 Madison Avenue
New York, NY 10021
212-734-3838
212-734-3165 (fax)

CRYSTAL

Baccarat
625 Madison Avenue
New York, NY 10022
800-777-0100, 212-826-4100
212-826-5043 (fax)

Christofle
680 Madison Avenue
New York, NY 10022
212-308-9390
212-644-7487 (fax)

CERAMICS AND COOKWARE

La Terrine
1024 Lexington Avenue
New York, NY 10021
212-988-3366

Camille Mizzi
248 Lafayette Street
New York, NY 10012
212-925-2484
212-274-1003 (fax)

Solanée (Ségriès)
866 Lexington Avenue
New York, NY 10021
212-439-6109
212-288-3065 (fax)

Le Cèdre Rouge
5, rue de Médicis
Paris 75006
42-33-71-05

22, avenue Victoria
Paris 75001
42-33-71-05
40-26-46-78 (fax)

Atelier du Cuivre
(Shown on pages 154–155)
54, rue Général Huard
50800 Villedieu-les-Poêles
France

33-51-31-85
33-51-04-96 (fax)
Workshop tours given daily; retail shop on the premises.

FABRICS

Edmond Petit
(Shown on page 31 are Brocatelle Louis XV and La Chasse. On page 32 (jacquard) are Fersen, Tourville, Damas Empire, Lampas Louis XVI)
23, rue du Mail
75081 Paris Cedex 02
42-33-48-56
40-26-24-56 (fax)

Edmond Petit fabrics also available at:
Andre Bon
D & D Building
979 Third Avenue, Room 606
New York, NY 10022
212-355-4012
212-888-6537 (fax)

Brunschwig
75 Virginia Road
P.O. Box 905
North White Plains,
NY 10606-0905
914-684-5800
914-684-0029 (fax)

Clarence House
111 Eighth Avenue, Space 801
New York, NY 10011
212-752-2890
212-645-8060 (fax)

Braquenié
(Petit point shown on page 33)
111 Boulevard Beaumarchais
75003 Paris
48-04-30-03
48-04-30-39 (fax)

Casa Lopez
(Petit point shown on page 33)
39-41 Galerie Vivienne
75002 Paris
42-60-83-70
42-60-56-26 (fax)

FLOWERS/DRIED FLOWERS

Many thanks for the flower arrangements on pages 110–111 to:

Christian Tortu
Carrefour de l'Odéon
75006 Paris
43-26-02-56
43-29-71-99 (fax)

Moulié Savart
8 Place du Palais Bourbon
75007 Paris
47-05-35-01
45-50-45-54 (fax)

Jules des Près
27 rue du Cherche Midi
75006 Paris

FRENCH CULTURE

The following is a list of schools and organizations that offer courses in French language, French newspapers and books, and various other cultural offerings.

Alliance Française
22 East 60 Street
New York, NY 10022
212-355-6100
212-935-4119 (fax)

810 North Dearborn Street
Chicago, IL 60610
312-337-1070

215 S. La Cienega Boulevard
Suite 104
Beverly Hills, CA 90211
310-652-0306

1345 Bush Street
San Francisco, CA 94109
415-775-7755
415-775-2539 (fax)

Or to find the Alliance Française nearest you, contact:
Fédération des Alliances Françaises
202-966-9740
202-362-1587 (fax)

Champs-Elysées
(One-hour news/entertainment programs on audiocassette)
446 Market Street
Nashville, TN 76444
615-338-9800

France Today
(A newspaper appearing 10 times a year written in English)
P.O. Box 1522
Martinez, CA 94553
800-851-7785

Journal Français d'Amérique
(A biweekly newspaper written in French)
P.O. Box 1522
Martinez, CA 94553
800-851-7785

Librairie de France
(French books, audiocassettes and learning guides)
610 Fifth Avenue
New York, NY 10002
212-581-8810

The Olivia and Hill Press
(French books on cassette)
905 Olivia Avenue
Ann Arbor, MI 48104
313-663-0235

For information on traveling to France, contact:
French Government Tourist Office
628 Fifth Avenue
New York, NY 10028
212-757-1125

MAIL ORDER

These mail-order companies offer a wide variety of French kitchenware, accessories, fabrics, and furnishings for the home. Call the 800 number provided for a catalog:

Joie de Vivre
800-648-8854

Rue de France
800-777-0998

Sur La Table
800-243-0852

L'Art de Vivre
800-411-6515

DECORATORS

The interior designs shown on pages 16–17, 18, 58–59, 60, 80, and 97 are by:

Corinne Wiley
Belvedere, CA
415-435-3218
415-435-0840 (fax)

The interior designs shown on pages 120–121 and 137 are by:

Paige Peterson
New York, NY
212-469-7529

INDEX